THE SPIRIT PATHS

OF

WALES

The remains of Narberth Castle

THE SPIRIT PATHS

OF

WALES

by

LAURENCE MAIN

This book is dedicated to the goddess Rhiannon

CICERONE PRESS
MILNTHORPE, CUMBRIA LA7 7PY
www.cicerone.co.uk

ACKNOWLEDGEMENTS

This book has come decades down a road along which many people have given me assistance. The great ley hunter Paul Devereux has been a major source of inspiration and encouragement, despite my words, no doubt, exasperating him at times. Danny Sullivan, Paul's successor as editor of *The Ley Hunter*, shared that burden to some extent. Meeting other ley hunters and listening to distinguished speakers at our annual Moots has also been a great privilege, especially when sharing walks with and sitting next to the likes of John Michell. Many people have contributed with the dreams I have tape-recorded when waking them from sleep at Carn Ingli and other sacred sites. Some have driven me to the more remote sites that were too difficult to reach by public transport. Special thanks are due to Philip Burton, Pat Caveille, Beck Cunningham, Ann Dunbar, John Dutton, Sarah Edwards, David Evans, Matthew Hill, Pamela Hopkinson, Claire Jenkins, Rev. Jim McKnight, Siân Meredudd, Betty Mungham-Harris, Joyce Nelson, Emma Orbach, Lisa Parfitt, Rosetta Reinke, Dill and Pete Revell, Letty Rowan, Charlie Sharp, Bronwen Thomas, Naomi Tydeman, Mickey Van der Helm-Hylkema, Dilys Walker, George Wemyss and Natasha Winn.

Advice to readers

Readers are advised that whilst every effort is taken by the author to ensure the accuracy of this guidebook, changes can occur which may affect the contents. It is advisable to check locally on transport, accommodation, shops etc, but even rights of way can be altered. The publishers would welcome notes of any such changes.

Front cover: *Pared y Cefnhir above Llynnau Cregennen*

CONTENTS

Page

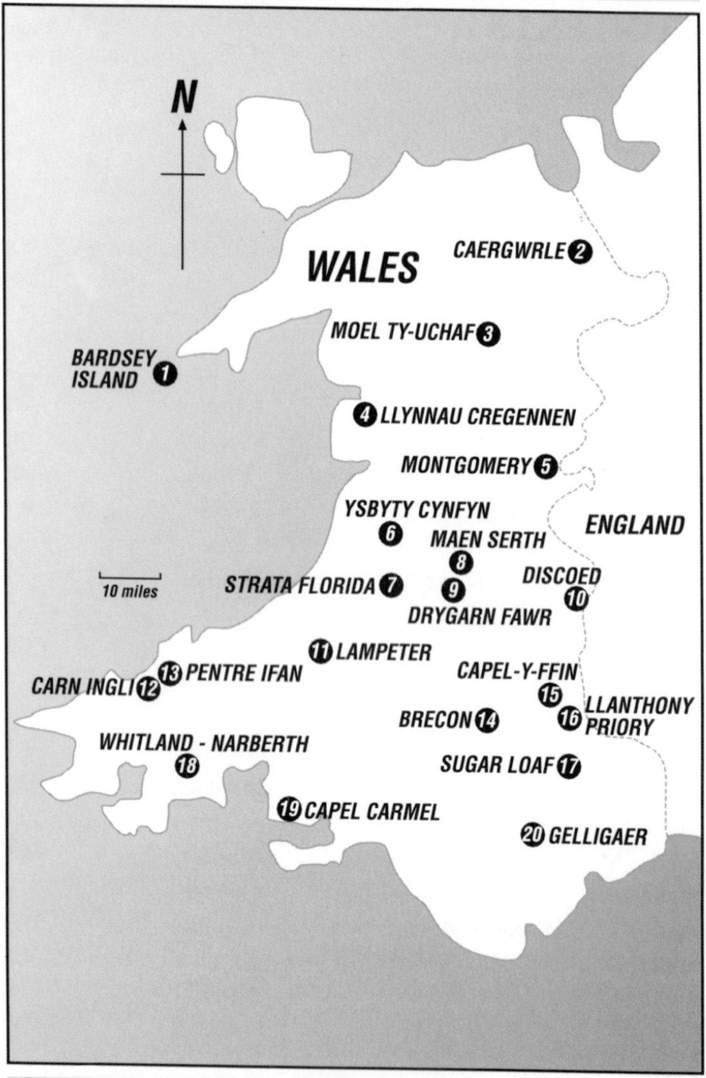

N

WALES

CAERGWRLE **2**

BARDSEY
ISLAND **1**

MOEL TY-UCHAF **3**

4 LLYNNAU CREGENNEN

MONTGOMERY **5**

YSBYTY CYNFYN
6

MAEN SERTH
8

ENGLAND

10 miles

STRATA FLORIDA **7**

9

DISCOED
10

DRYGARN FAWR

11 LAMPETER

CARN INGLI **12** **13** PENTRE IFAN

CAPEL-Y-FFIN

15 **16** LLANTHONY
PRIORY

BRECON **14**

WHITLAND - NARBERTH
18

SUGAR LOAF **17**

19 CAPEL CARMEL

20 GELLIGAER

③	*The walking route with distance walked from the start in miles and direction of walk*
......	*Other path (not necessarily a right of way)*
	Track
= = =	*Motor road*
≡	*Railway*
	Railway station
	Hedge or fence
↟↟↟	*Wall*
━	*Standing stone, rock or pond*
•	*Stone circle*
∵	*Gate*
G	*Stile*
S	*Signpost*
P	
→	*Stream or river, with direction of flow*
⇥⇤	*Bridge*
■	*Building*
-	*Ruin*
⠐ⁿ⠐	*Ruined church, large mound, Roman practice camp*
Ⴈ	*Lighthouse*
▵	*Summit, cairn*
♠ ♀	*Trees*
⟩⟋	*Steep, dangerous crags*
⁝⁝⁝	*Earthwork, hillfort*
♡	*Lake*
⋒	*Burial chamber*
⋈	*Tumulus*
⊓	*Castle*
+	*Church*
Ⴟ	*Campsite*
•────→	*Spirit path, ley*
⠒⠒⠒⠒	*Course of dismantled railway*
⊥ N	*Direction of north*

Each map has a scale in miles and a gradient profile showing the height in feet and the distance in miles from the start.

Afon is Welsh for river. Nant means stream.

INTRODUCTION

Spirit paths, *leys* or *ley lines* are new concepts to many people who have come to enjoy walking in the countryside. They form part of that ancestral memory of being the children of Mother Earth which makes so many town-dwellers yearn for the simple freedom of rambling along ancient paths. This vital contact with the living landscape is a spiritual exercise.

What is meant by a ley, or spirit path, is very much open to individual interpretation. Significantly, it is a straight path or track that is identified in one's subconscious and is consequently traced by a process of dowsing and connecting sight-lines. The paths often synchronise with standing stones, holy wells and other sacred sites, suggesting a divine or mystical significance. A ley has variously been described as a 'straight line of light', an 'alignment of ancient sites', a 'straight track through the countryside', an 'energy stream across the earth', a 'cult road', or quite simply a 'legend, revelation or vision'. Those who have studied the subject, such as Alfred Watkins or Paul Devereux, give their own interpretations, which are described in more detail below.

My personal journey began with walking ancient routes and visiting many enigmatic prehistoric monuments. An excellent public library service fanned these initial flames, but books, however good, came second to my personal acquaintance with the land through rambling. Sleeping and dreaming at sacred sites and dowsing what I see in my mind as straight lines of light, like sunbeams, and which I call leys or spirit paths, seemed to follow quite naturally. This is very much a personal, subjective, thing. Test the reality of it by doing it for yourselves.

A significant year was 1970, when I first discovered the Ridgeway (in particular, Uffington white horse) and when a book that had first been published in 1925 was reprinted. This is *The Old Straight Track* by Alfred Watkins and it is still the work with which to begin a study of what Watkins terms leys and which I now prefer to call spirit paths.

This statue at Capel-y-ffin's Monastery commemorates the visions of the Virgin Mary seen in 1880

In a foreword to the new edition of Watkins' book, John Michell, the author of another seminal book, *The View Over Atlantis* (first published in 1969 and fully revised in 1983 with the title *The New View Over Atlantis*), wrote of the revelation Watkins had when riding across the hills of his native Herefordshire. A vision granted Watkins the privilege of perceiving the network of leys in 'a single flash'. This was at a time when the archaeological establishment wouldn't credit our ancestors with the ability to survey alignments accurately. As Michell wrote, Watkins was 'a true gnostic in that he preferred the evidence of his own senses and the voice of his own intuition to the unsupported evidence of authority'. Watkins wrote of the alignment of ancient sites, for which he used the term *ley*, with its archaic meanings of clearing and surveying the land. He thought of leys as primitive trackways, although not like surfaced roads. Sections of roads do conform to leys (and it is clear that the Romans took credit for laying out routes of much greater antiquity), but Watkins' routes are essentially a series of marker points to be aimed at. A sight-line would be taken on a distant peak, then a mound or tumulus placed on an intermediate ridge. The actual track may swerve from the straight line, especially in difficult terrain, but would be sure to converge with the ley at important crossroads or fords. Stones marked the way and were, perhaps, dedicated to *Mercury* and assisted *merch*ants to reach their *mark*ets. Mercury could be equated with Hermes, the messenger of the gods and guide both to wayfarers on unknown pathways and the souls of the dead seeking the Otherworld. Hermits would live at strategic points, rendering both material and spiritual assistance to wayfarers. In the same mould was the Egyptian Thoth, becoming the Celtic Toutates or Toot. The Welsh word for a sighting-mound is *twt* (pronounced 'toot').

Some standing stones evolved into wayside crosses, while Christian churches were built on much older sacred sites. Sacred trees and holy wells were significant, while water sighting-points included lakes and artificial moats which could reflect light from beacons. Skyline notches were aimed for on hills, while leys tended to glance the edges of hillforts or camps.

Particular names are associated with the laying-out of these tracks. *Cole* is derived from the ancient word for diviner, sorcerer or wizard. The Welsh word *coel* means omen. This could be corrupted to *cold* (nothing to do with being chilly). *Dod* is a reference to the early surveyors' sighting staffs, which were akin to the two horns on the head of a snail or dodman, as Watkins realised at Llanthony (see Route 16). *Black* (or *Blake*) is another such name, ironically derived from 'shining, white, pale' as in 'bleach'. Of course, the man who lit the beacon could both give light and have a grimy appearance. Beacon hills are often initial points of leys, beckoning travellers towards them. The beacons would have been invaluable to the early surveyors. Related words are *Tan* (Welsh for fire, sometimes rendered as St Anne) and *Brent* (burnt).

Folk memories of the straight passages through the countryside, particularly involving castles and churches, would become tunnel legends. The sites would also become traditional places of assembly.

John Michell took up Watkins' leys in his broader view of an archaic, divine, global system, encompassing sacred measurements and the mystical code of number. His *View Over Atlantis* encouraged the acceptance of 'energy streams across the earth'. This planet is to be regarded as a vessel for the alchemical fusion between solar or cosmic energies and the earth spirit. Leys are also linked to UFOs or 'flying saucers', whose appearance Jung identified as portending a change in our attitudes and perceptions, heralding the New Age of Aquarius. Watkins had hinted at such conclusions himself, mentioning Hermes and quoting the Bible:

> 'Thus saith the Lord, Stand ye in the ways, and see, and ask for the old paths, where is the good way, and walk therein, and ye shall find rest for your souls.'
> (Jeremiah vi 16)

As things stood in the 1920s (when the editor of *Antiquity* notoriously refused even a paid advertisement for Watkins' *Old Straight Track*), the time was not then ripe to expand on the spiritual side of leys. By the end of the 1960s, John Michell was able to go beyond the notion of tracks to the forgotten principle behind the siting of sacred centres. Geometrical patterns emerged and astronomical links with significant positions of the sun and moon were noted (before archaeologists recognised these at ancient monuments). Leys were entering the magical realms of a lost universal culture, the fabled Atlantis.

Cup-marked stones (as on Route 20, Gelligaer) are reckoned to be maps of both the stars in the sky and patterns of sites on the land laid out to reflect them. Stone circles serve as receiving stations for the cosmic currents (much as the dream, recorded on Carn Ingli, of Rhiannon's fingers recounted in Route 3 suggests). Leys become the nervous system or acupuncture meridians of a landscape giant, channelling seasonal fertility.

Describing leys as 'spiritual paths', Michell compared them to the *lung-mei* or dragon paths of China and the fairy paths of Ireland. One great dragon path recognised as running from Cornwall to Norfolk is a line described in greater detail by Hamish Miller and Paul Broadhurst in their 1989 book *The Sun and the Serpent*. This great ley was traced across the width of the country with the aid of dowsing rods.

The second of two standing stones before the forestry plantation overlooking Barmouth - Route 4

I had first come across dowsing by reading Guy Underwood's book *The Pattern of the Past* (again, first published in 1969), the works of T.C. Lethbridge (notably *The Power of the Pendulum*) and Tom Graves (including *Needles of Stone*, republished as *Needles of Stone*

Revisited). Dowsing, like dreaming, was something other people did until I met the dowser with the Dragon Project at the Rollrights, where I also dreamt on the edge of the stone circle, in March 1980. She kindly lent me her dowsing rods and suggested I use them to find a ley. Thinking of a shining path or sunbeam and mentally asking for a ley, I soon dowsed a line. My mentor then unrolled her map to show that I had dowsed the same ley as she had marked on it. I soon bought my own dowsing rods and found they worked.

This is where the personal, subjective, nature of seeking spirit paths comes in. I still can't think of myself as knowing much about dowsing, or dreaming, yet I have come to practise both when dealing with leys or spirit paths and the sacred sites visited by them. They appeal to my intuition and my motivation is high when employing them for my specific purposes. It's a bit like having a radio permanently tuned into one wavelength. When I turn on the knob, the reception is good, but I don't know much about the radio. I don't want to know, or treat them as toys or for finding wonders. They are old friends that help me do a job.

Taking my dowsing rods to, say, a standing stone, I ask them to show me where the primary ley or most important spirit path is. I hold the image of a shining path in my mind. Walking slowly around the stone, I stop when my rods cross. This is the first edge of the spirit path. Taking another step or two will bring me to the second edge of it. Spirit paths are usually four or five feet wide (the width does seem to change according to season and phase of the moon). I then mark these two edges, usually with sticks.

Completing my circle, I repeat the process where the line comes out on the other side of the stone. I then walk in increasingly bigger circles round it to mark the dowsed line further from the stone. Selecting just one edge of the spirit path (beware of confusing the two edges!), I stand on it and face north.

Taking out my hand-held Silva compass, I turn its housing so that it is aligned with the dowsed line I am standing on. The arrow of the compass points north, where I am facing. I can now take the compass bearing of the spirit path. Let's say it is 54 degrees. I deduct four degrees for magnetic variation, giving the actual bearing of this line on the map at 50 degrees. (The difference between magnetic north, grid north and true north varies from time and place, so check it in the key to your Ordnance Survey map.) Already we are dealing in approximates. Nevertheless, I walk to the other side of the stone and to the second edge of the spirit path to repeat the process and check the accuracy of this bearing.

My method can't be too far from the technological capability of Watkins' dodmen with their sighting staffs. Perhaps the coleman had divined the ley for them, while Mr Blake attended to the beacon on the hill ahead which would assist the process.

Now comes the moment of revelation. Firstly, look up and down the dowsed line to see what appears on the horizons and intermediate points. You may have the satisfaction of a notch in a hill or a succession of aligned gateways in a series of fields. Secondly, open the map and carefully draw the dowsed line on it (in pencil, with a ruler). Bingo! You've hit a significant point, perhaps another standing stone. If it is the only other standing stone marked on that map, the odds on you finding it are staggering. Maybe you have dowsed the same line as another ley hunter. If this is so, isn't this confirmation of it?

Allow for some fine tuning to your line, if it appears obviously needed. Accuracy within a degree or two is good in the circumstances. I tend to trust my initial finding, based on intuition and invocation. Enjoy that glow of authentic satisfaction when, as I did at the Great Oak Stone near Crickhowell (Route 17), you hit the jackpot first time and without the potential influence of having any clues to its direction.

Now devise a walking route using rights of way giving access to the spirit path. Dowse as you go along, or at least when the map tells you that you are approaching the spirit path again. Put the map away and concentrate on dowsing. When your rods cross, open the map again and check that you are on the line dowsed at the start. Confirm its compass bearing. Repeat this process until the end of the walk, with a second standing stone, perhaps, as your destination. If you have dowsed the same line throughout, isn't it right to conclude that it is a spirit path?

The hardest thing, I find, is cutting out the other leys (you can go down the scale, secondary and so on) at the start. Your rods will want to cross for them too but, to avoid confusion, ask firmly for the primary ley and only the primary ley. Once tuned in to the desired ley, you'll probably find you can dowse it at intervals along the way without rods (I receive a thump in the head when I cross the ley). Pulled up short, you can then check it with rods, compass and map.

Note the bearing for significant alignments. Since starting this book I've discovered (thanks to a dreamer lending me *The First Stonehenge* by Gaynor Francis) that 50 degrees is the angle of the summer solstice sunrise, for instance. I did not know when I originally walked and dowsed at Moel Ty-uchaf (Route 3) that moonset in northerly major standstill is 320 degrees. My ignorance

Maen Serth - Route 8

became bliss when I realised how close my dowsed line at a bearing of 319 degrees obviously corresponds to it. When I dowsed it, I was just amazed to find it led to the cairn on the summit of Cadair Bronwen.

So much for dowsing, which I first tried when visiting the Dragon Project. This research project was organised by *The Ley*

Hunter, a magazine produced on a voluntary basis but with a professional reputation. Its editor for 20 years, from 1976, was the man who, as a self-employed writer, has done the most research into leys, Paul Devereux.

Devereux's thorough study of his subject bore its first fruit in the form of a book with the publication of *The Ley Hunter's Companion* (co-author Ian Thomson) in 1979, later republished as *The Ley Guide*. After going back over the work of Watkins and Michell, Devereux tackled the more fanciful of his ley hunting contemporaries, pointing out that the scale of the map and the thickness of the pencil, let alone the curvature of the earth, made it necessary to concentrate on short leys. Facing the problem of academic recognition, he set out to gain it. As Robert Forrest's work with statistics showed, this approach can bring problems. 'How many times must a baby be born before it is statistically considered to have arrived?', asked Devereux. The reality of leys was furnished with examples from home and abroad, including the *ceques* of Peru. Devereux revealed his UFO background by describing a light he saw in the sky in 1967. His next book, published in 1982, was *Earth Lights*. It was followed by *Earth Lights Revelation* (1989). Confounding the 'nuts and bolts' flying saucer brigade, he showed that there were strange lights in the sky, but of the earth and related to fault lines. Stone circles and leys correlated with these. Again, personal experience is so vital. This was of little interest to me until I witnessed earthlights on Carn Ingli three nights running in November 1996. It wasn't until after the third night that I dared to tell a friend at the foot of this sacred peak. Contacting Paul Devereux, he confirmed there had been an 'outbreak' of earthlights at that time.

Combining with Nigel Pennick (whose book *The Ancient Science of Geomancy* was published in 1979) to write *Lines on the Landscape* (1989), Devereux commented how 'the ley theory, at first glance so innocuous, seems to touch some sort of cultural nerve in modern thinking'. Our relationship with the land, our perception of our ancestors, even our spirituality were all called into question. Considering leys as energy lines, however, Devereux questions the basis of the theory, concluding that 'the dowsing rod has become an implement to authorise the acceptance of subjective ideas as factual statements'.

Naive New Agers flashing crystals, practising manipulation at powerpoints and proclaiming global energy grids for which they have little or no proof have given dowsed leys a bad name. They are the wrong image when academic respectability is being courted. Unfortunately, this rejection of dowsing runs the risk of throwing the baby out with the bath-water. Dowsing need not be, as Devereux fears, a projection onto the land. It can and should be a learning from it.

It is the final chapter of *Lines on the Landscape* that took ley research into a new stage. Not that old Alfred Watkins hadn't mentioned Hermes as being the 'leader over unknown trackways of departed souls to the nether world'. Devereux had latched on to the passage of spirits.

Straightness, a fundamental feature of leys (at least it used to be, but let's keep this simple), is associated with the divine and with the divine representatives on earth, kings. In the introduction to our joint book *The Old Straight Tracks of Wessex* (Devereux and Main, 1992) Devereux explains that the Indo-European root word *reg* meant 'movement along a straight line'. Right, direction, regular, correct, regulate, regiment, regal, reign and rule are all examples stemming from this. Does not the word 'ruler' mean both a straight edge and a king? Lines radiating from the seat of power (as with the Golden Throne in the Forbidden City at Beijing, or the Inca Temple of the Sun in Cuzco) can be seen as channels for the royal spirit - as spirit paths.

If, as J.G. Frazer wrote in *The Golden Bough* (1922), 'the king is the lineal successor of the old magician', were these spirit paths used by shamans for out-of-body flight? And what of the spirits of the dead? A prime example of a spirit path for the dead is the Viking 'cult road' at Rosaring, Sweden. More examples from continental Europe, the 'death roads' of the Netherlands and the 'ghost roads' of Germany, appeared in Devereux's subsequent books *Symbolic Landscapes* and *Shamanism and the Mystery Lines* (both 1992).

Paul Devereux signed off as editor of *The Ley Hunter* in the winter issue of 1995/96 with a blast against the lunatic fringe of energy line dowsers. His grounding of the subject has brought it into the arena of 'consciousness studies'. A younger breed of archaeologists is more open-minded to leys. This new orthodoxy was repeated in an editorial by Devereux's successor, Danny Sullivan, in *The Ley Hunter* no. 128. My *Walks in Mysterious Oxfordshire* was described as an 'otherwise useful walking guide peppered with references to energy dowsing, dowsable ley lines and the "Drowsers' Bible", *The Sun and the Serpent*'. The witch-finder-general must have been a bit like that.

That issue of *The Ley Hunter* appeared at the 20th anniversary Moot, the annual gathering of ley hunters, in 1997. That Saturday morning in Wiltshire I turned on Radio 4's early morning news to hear that (and I paraphrase) 'hundreds of ley hunters are converging on Avebury', followed by illuminating interviews. Danny Sullivan spoke of how leys or spirit paths were gaining academic respectability because the movement was shedding its energy-line image and researching 'dead straight' coffin paths. A very respectable academic was then asked what he thought of leys, only to disappoint by stating that he was far too busy studying more important things to consider them. Then, as time ran out, the radio interviewer gladdened my heart by adding a final twist to the tale. She said that she knew leys were real because she had been dowsing them with a friend at Stonehenge recently.

We are back to the personal, subjective, nature of dowsing spirit paths. After the lectures that day, most Moot-goers retired to the pub, perhaps to talk over theories on leys. It was a full moon and I preferred to take the opportunity to sleep under it on Silbury Hill. I had been walking the footpaths and dowsing the leys of Wiltshire for the previous fortnight, so I felt 'in tune' with the land. I wanted to listen to and be with it. That night a gang of drunken hooligans came up to desecrate this holy spot, including throwing a firework at one point. I rose up naked from my sleeping-bag and told them to clear off. The shock made them do so (fortunately). That night I dreamt I was wearing white robes and bore a staff. It was the night of a full moon and I was one of a circle of such figures at Stonehenge, keeping the masses back from the clear inner sanctuary.

The next morning's *Observer* had an article about the Moot and how the new ley hunters craved respectability, while 'behind the scenes plots are being hatched to rid the movement of its more eccentric figures'. Autumn 1997 saw an article in *3rd Stone* by Danny Sullivan advocating coffin paths and the conceptual rather than physical invisible spirit roads of shamanic flight and the Kogi Indians of Colombia. Watkins didn't recognise what he saw. There is no such thing as a ley. 'It is time to bury the ley.'

So the wise men have spoken and who is to argue? There'll be plenty to do that. Alby Stone has already weighed in with his book *Straight Track, Crooked Road: Leys, Spirit Paths and Shamanism* (1998).

Read *The Ley Hunter*, if you can. Sadly, it has temporarily ceased publication, though a revival is planned. (To acquire a copy please contact the author via Cicerone Press.) Acquire your own dowsing rods (The Centre for Alternative Technology, Machynlleth, Powys SY20 9AZ sells them), buy a good compass and those most valuable keys to the countryside, the Ordnance Survey maps (Pathfinder maps are being replaced with Explorers) and walk the spirit paths yourselves. Details of the Ramblers in Wales are available from Ty'r Cerddwyr, High Street, Gresford, Wrecsam LL12 8PT.

Late 1999 saw the publication of a book by the last editor of *The Ley Hunter* magazine. Danny Sullivan's *Ley Lines* reaffirmed its author's belief in leys. This book also announced the formation of The Society of Ley Hunters, PO Box 1634, Hassocks BN6 8BZ. An excellent little book also published in 1999 was *Leylines* by Philip Heselton, founder editor of *The Ley Hunter* magazine in 1965.

Spirit paths have been the subject of much debate as, inevitably, the human mind attempts to reduce to words, even dogma, what belongs to a greater sphere than we can envisage. Cynics claim that they are the product of our own imagination, though perhaps it is their own blinkers that prevent the light from shining in. People who are ruled by fear don't want to know about spirit. Our minds act as filters and erect barriers to things that threaten our belief structures. We can perceive such subliminal information in our dreams, however, while a positive attitude counts for much, as does a relaxed open-mindedness and a child-like concentration. This is an acceptance of the spark of divinity within each soul. Becoming aware of the subconscious is easier in the country, away from desensitising city life.

This book has a selection of spirit paths (by my reckoning) for you to sample. It is far from being comprehensive. I've just dipped into a vast ocean. I hope I haven't imposed my dowsed lines on the land. I tried to listen to it. If I may venture a belief, it is that this is a living land and our acknowledgement of its spirit paths may lead us to love it.

Laurence Main

Distance:	5 miles
Start:	The Boathouse, grid ref.: SH 116211
OS Maps:	Explorer 12 (Lleyn Peninsula West), Landranger 123 (Lleyn Peninsula)

Public Transport

Take the ferry to Bardsey from Pwllheli. Pwllheli is the northern terminus of the Cambrian Coast line with trains from Birmingham and Machynlleth (tel. 0345 484950). Buses to Pwllheli include no. 3 from Porthmadog and no. 12 from Caernarfon. It is possible to take the ferry from Porth Meudwy (SH 163255) near Aberdaron. Bus no. 17 runs to Aberdaron from Pwllheli. Tel. 01286 679535 for bus times. The weekly boat should sail on Saturdays, but be prepared for delays caused by bad weather. This is a real pilgrimage!

Accommodation

Day trips may be possible on fine summer days but plan to stay on Bardsey for at least one week (your return trip may be delayed by bad weather), booking well in advance and bringing supplies not listed as being provided on the island when you book. Camping is not allowed but the accommodation offers good value. The Bardsey Bird and Field Observatory offers hostel accommodation: book through Mrs Alicia Normand, BBFO Bookings Secretary, 46 Maudlin Drive, Teignmouth, Devon TQ14 8SB, tel. 01626 773908, or you could rent a house on a self-catering basis through Simon Glyn, Director, The Bardsey Island Trust, Coed Anna, Nanhoron, Pwllheli, Gwynedd LL53 8PR, tel. 01758 730740.

Introduction

Of all the islands which fringe the Welsh coast, Bardsey is the most sanctified. Here is a real Isle of the Blessed in the West, an island for the dead situated at the end of a peninsula along which a concentration of spirit paths and ancient pilgrims' ways run. Corpses were brought here by boat from across Cardigan Bay. The bodies of the dead were recorded as being laid to rest in the ancient church on the sands at Llandanwg, south of Harlech, before being brought on the hazardous sea journey to be buried on Bardsey. In the Middle Ages, three pilgrimages to Bardsey were deemed to equal one to Rome.

Why this obsession with the dead and an island at the tip of a peninsula? It seems to be international. My mind recalls a true ghost story recorded by Sir Arthur Grimble in *A Pattern of Islands*. The Gilbert Islands are a fairly straight string of islands in the western half of the Pacific Ocean and lying on the equator, about one thousand miles east of the Solomon Islands. Makin Meang, the northernmost of the Gilbert Islands, is considered the 'halfway house between the lands of the living and the dead'.

Grimble, who worked as a British colonial officer on the islands, noted a belief which he reckoned to be at least 60 generations old that the souls of the dead travelled northwards on a straight line to a sandspit on a shore of Makin Meang. Known as the Place of Dread and the Gate of Death, souls departed from here over the western horizon for the 'lands of ancient desire', eventually reaching the Gilbertese heaven of Matang. This lost Eden can now only be glimpsed in dreams. Te Kaetikawai is a ritual given to the Gilbertese long ago by Nakaa the Judge, who sits at the gate of Death at Makin Meang. The ritual involves following a straight line and souls who wander off this are ensnared with a net and a pit. Despite native protestations, Grimble insisted on being taken to the Place of Dread. Having visited the sandspit, Grimble walked back, southwards, along the path towards the village. This meant he would meet any spirits making their way to the northern tip of the island. Becoming thirsty, Grimble desired a coconut from a tree. He hadn't learned how to climb one himself, so he asked an old man with a scar and a limp who was coming from the village towards him. This was about 3pm. 'He totally ignored the greeting I gave him. He did not even turn his eyes towards me. He went by as if I didn't exist .... I was shocked speechless. It was so grossly unlike the infallible courtesy of the islanders', Grimble recalled. Reaching the village, Grimble discovered that he had met the ghost of a man who had died that afternoon, shortly before 3pm. His body was still in the village.

So in Wales we have spirit paths converging on the tip of Llŷn (Lleyn Peninsula) off which is Bardsey Island with the reputed graves of 20,000 saints. Myrddin (Merlin) is also said to be sleeping on Bardsey in a glass castle. Here he guards the 13 treasures of Britain, being Arthur's Cloak of Invisibility, the Sword of Rhydderch Hael, the Hamper of Gwyddno Garanhir, the Drinking Horn of Bran, the Chariot of Morgan, the Halter of Clydno Eiddyn, the Knife of Llawfrodedd, the Cauldron of Dyrnwch, the Whetstone of Tudwal Tydglyd, the Red Coat of Padarn, the board game Gwyddbwll, the Ring of Eluned and the dish of Rhygenydd. (*The Welsh Triads* also list the Crock of Rhygenydd and the Mantle of Tegau Gold-Breast - making 15.) Which Myrddin is this? Bearing in mind that we are dealing with a title and an archetype rather than

Trwyn Maen Melyn (Yellow Stone Point) overlooking Bardsey Island

an individual (other Myrddins are buried or kept captive elsewhere), could this be St Dyfrig, the Archbishop of Caerleon who crowned the young Arthur in AD 497 at Woodchester, in the year of the comet and the death of Ambrosius Aurelianus (Emrys Wledig - Myrddin Emrys)? He was buried on Bardsey but his remains were later transferred to Llandaff Cathedral, Cardiff. Ironically, given the lengths that others were taken to be buried on Bardsey, a gravestone bearing the earliest example of Welsh writing (c. AD 600) kept in St Cadfan's Church, Tywyn, may suggest that St Cadfan, who founded the Celtic Christian community on Bardsey and is counted as its first abbot, lies buried between four markstones in the churchyard at Tywyn, Meirionydd, and not on Bardsey. His successor, Lleuddad, was buried on the island, as was a later (the third?) abbot, Derfel, the former warrior associated with Camlan who became a saint and probably died around 570. Derfel, too, was a Myrddin.

This sixth century 'monastery' (not at all like the Roman Catholic monasteries of the Middle Ages) had its spiritual centre on the site occupied in the Middle Ages by the Augustinian monastery dedicated to St Mary. The surviving tower may be Celtic. In a dream whilst on the island, I saw Derfel Gadarn inside this tower, where there is still a makeshift altar. Abbot Derfel's grave lies a few feet south of the tower, according to my dowsing rods.

When 1200 monks of Bangor-is-y-coed (near Wrexham) were slaughtered by the Saxons at the Battle of Chester early in the seventh century, 900 survivors were said to have fled to Bardsey. How did they all fit on this tiny island? Perhaps they followed the straight (spirit path?) route running west from Bangor-is-y-coed to Clynog Fawr and detailed in *The Trackway of the Cross* by Alan Shore. Before their coming, in Derfel's time, the majority of the population seems to have lived in huts just below the 548ft summit of Mynydd Enlli, with more huts clustered along the northern coastline and a few at the southern end, near where the lighthouse sends out its beam today.

The Welsh name for Bardsey Island is Ynys Enlli, which may refer to the strong currents which make it so difficult to reach by boat from the mainland or to Fenlli or Benlli, a local prince who may have lived in the fifth century and been deposed by St Germanus, presumably because he was a Pelagian heretic. The Saxons may have called the island after its Bards or Bardsey may be a Viking name. The island certainly feels Druidical and Pelagian rather than Roman and Catholic. Pelagius was the 20th abbot of Bangor-is-y-coed who nobly stood for the original teachings of Jesus as given directly to the Druids, including an acceptance of reincarnation, the importance of individual conscience and freewill, the law of cause and effect and the power of good works. These did not suit the political power of the papacy in Rome, whose new dogmas allowed the institution of the Church to rule through fear, whilst the bishops and popes set their store in earthly riches. For defending the ancient, simple, faith, Pelagius was described as a heretic by Rome and 'St' Germanus of Auxerre was sent on a mission to bring Britain into line in the fifth century. Roman patriarchy determined to wipe out the more feminine spirituality of the Celts.

Bardsey has been identified as the Isle of Afallach. Afallach is Avallon, being the Island of Apples. Apples are still grown on Bardsey and such trees would have flourished before the introduction of sheep in the Middle Ages (now the danger of liver fluke is so great that it isn't safe to eat the watercress which formed the staple part of the Celtic saints' diet - some were vegan).

As Chris Barber and David Pykitt point out in their book *Journey to Avalon*, Geoffrey of Monmouth's 'Insula Afallonis' was rendered 'Ynys Afallach' in Welsh versions of his manuscript. Welsh Druidical tradition places this Island of Apples off Cardigan Bay in the direction of Ireland. Interestingly, it is also called 'Fortunate' - the 'Insula pomorum que Fortunata' to which Myrddin (Merlin) and Taliesin took the mortally wounded Arthur. In a dream on the battlefield of Camlan on the anniversary of the battle (23rd June, not allowing for the change in the calendar) a few days after visiting Bardsey Island in 1998, but before I knew of its description as 'Fortunate', I had a vivid picture of an island which appeared to be Bardsey and said, in my dream, that it was 'Hope Island'.

The mortally wounded Arthur was taken to Afallach/ Avalon/Bardsey after the Battle of Camlan (probably in AD 537). Camlan was fought near Dinas Mawddwy, about 10 miles east of Dolgellau. Perhaps Arthur's body was taken by boat from Arthog in the Mawddach Estuary. The dying solar king was to be taken for healing to Morgan Le Fay and her nine maidens. Bardsey is here linked with a lunar/goddess aspect. Camlan was fought because Arthur had been used by Illtyd's Roman patriarchal party to go against Gwynedd, Celtic spirituality and the goddess. Malory has Morgan Le Fay married to Urien of Gorre in his *Le Morte d'Arthur*. *The Welsh Triads* have Urien of Gorre married to Modron (the Mother Goddess), the daughter of Afallach. It is also recorded that Rhun the son of Maelgwn Gwynedd (whose kingdom Arthur attempted and failed to invade at Camlan) was also the grandson of Afallach (his mother Gwalltwen being Afallach's daughter and the concubine of Maelgwn). Perhaps the reference to a glass castle is Modron/Morgan Le Fay's primitive greenhouse on what is, potentially, a fertile island (now sadly overgrazed by sheep).

Dowsing for the most important spirit path on Bardsey, I found it to run at an angle of about 30 degrees through the lighthouse and the tower that survives at the site of St Mary's Abbey. This line forms an axis through the island. Looking along this line from the northern end of the island brought the summit of Mynydd Anelog into focus on the mainland. This is extremely interesting. A retired GP on Llŷn, Dr D.T. Lloyd Hughes, has done some amazing independent research on straight lines which he calls straths and I would call leys or spirit paths. These have two focal points at the western end of the peninsula. The first is at St Mary's in Uwchmynydd. At grid ref. SH 139253, this is now ruined. There is still a path to a curious holy well in a gully below the church. This is covered by the sea at high tide, yet contains fresh water from a spring at low tide. Legend requires of pilgrims that they fill their mouths with water from this well and run three times around the church without dropping or swallowing a drop, whilst making a wish. This was the final target for pilgrims before sailing from the mainland for Bardsey. This holy well is called Ffynnon Mair, emphasising the feminine nature of this place. Above it stands an unusual stone called Maen Melyn (Yellow Stone - it is covered with yellowish moss) at Trwyn Maen Melyn (Yellow Stone Point). The most important spirit path dowsed here is aligned with the stone's curious 'finger'. This goes inland to the old church on the sands at Aberdaron, dedicated to St Hynwyn (whose mother was King Arthur's sister Gwenonwy). It is possible to extend this line eastwards to Criccieth Castle. I count this as a 'feminine' spirit path.

The other focus is what I consider to be 'masculine'. It is the summit of Mynydd Anelog (Aiming Mountain - what a name!). A chapel once stood on this hillside. An extension of the axis spirit path I dowsed on Bardsey leads through St Mary's to Mynydd Anelog!

If 'female' straths converge on St Mary's and 'male' straths aim for Mynydd Anelog, the most important spirit path running through Bardsey and linking with these points on the mainland could be seen as drawing on both energies, encouraging synthesis, balance and harmony. This was the Celtic Druidical ideal, unlike that of a patriarchal church that still refuses to admit women to its priesthood.

It is time to consider an important little booklet by Robin Heath: *A Key to Stonehenge*. This is more concerned with two other holy islands, Caldey and Lundy, both near the mouth of the Bristol Channel and at about the same longitude (4 degrees 41 minutes west of Greenwich). Read *A Key to Stonehenge* to realise how this is all to do with male/female harmony. Bardsey Island is slightly west of this significant line, being about 4 degrees 47 minutes (similar to St Brynach's Church, Nevern, Pembrokeshire). Mynydd Anelog is closer at about 4 degrees 44 minutes, while the important church dedicated to St Hynwyn on the sands at Aberdaron is about spot on at 4 degrees 42 minutes and Castell Odo (SH 187284) is another significant point almost exactly on the magical 4 degrees and 41 minutes west of Greenwich. Caldey, Lundy, Stonehenge and Carn Menyn, the source of the Bluestones in the Preselis, fit into gigantic landscape geometrical patterns. Do Bardsey and the tip of Llŷn further up the line to the north?

Route
(Mile 0) Face the slipway and landing stage on the sheltered eastern side of Bardsey Island, on the northern side of the bay inhabited by about 100 seals (watch them bask and sing on the rocks in the sunshine at low tide). Go right to walk around the coastline in a clockwise direction, keeping the sea on your left and the lighthouse on your right. Go to the extreme southern tip, where the atmosphere is especially otherworldly and there are traces of an ancient hut circle **(Mile 1)**.

Continue through the same gateway as you came through when entering this southern end of the island. Walk with a beach on your left (the wilder, western, shore). Go ahead over a stile to walk with a wall on your right **(Mile 2)**.

Continue with the sea on your left and through a gate ahead. Reach the northern shore and go right, keeping the sea on your left **(Mile 3)**.

Approach a stile in the fence ahead marking the start of the steep hillside which forms the eastern side of most of the island. Do not cross this stile. Turn right, inland, to walk with a wall on your left and enter a walled field. Leave by its far right corner and bear right through a gate to walk with a fence and shelter belt of conifer trees on your left. Turn left at the corner to follow a wall on your left and reach a cluster of buildings with the surviving tower of the ruined St Mary's Abbey ahead on your left. Visit this, return to the track junction and go right to pass the abbey ruins on your right and head for the steep hillside. An easy, broad, grassy track bears right to pass the Methodist chapel on your right. Only take this if the wind is too strong to enjoy the more rugged climb where you start by bearing left, then go right to reach the 548ft summit of Mynydd Enlli. The climb may be strenuous but the views are superb on a clear day (especially if you have binoculars - usually available from somebody on the island). The forked prongs of the Rivals (Yr Eifl), easily distinguished at the north-eastern end of Llyn, hide the higher Carneddau. Snowdon can be made out, yet hemmed in by other peaks. Much more outstanding, as your gaze sweeps southwards down the coastline of Cardigan Bay, after the Rhinog range, is the great bulk of Cadair Idris. This is a splendid mountain from so many directions inland, but looking at Cadair Idris across the sea from Bardsey hammers home the power of this peak. On a fine day you can see right down to Pembrokeshire (try and pick out Carn Ingli, then when on Carn Ingli look north for Bardsey at the end of Llŷn). The Wicklow Mountains beckon on the western side of the Irish Sea, while Holyhead Mountain and the Isle of Anglesey can be seen in the north **(Mile 4)**.

Continue southwards, keeping safely above the sea on your left, to pass a rock which is shaped like a frog (and through which seems to run a roughly east-west spirit path). Keep a wall on your right as you descend, bear right through a gap to cut a corner and pass gorse bushes on your right. Go ahead through a gate and walk with the bay and its seals on your left back to the boathouse **(Mile 5)**.

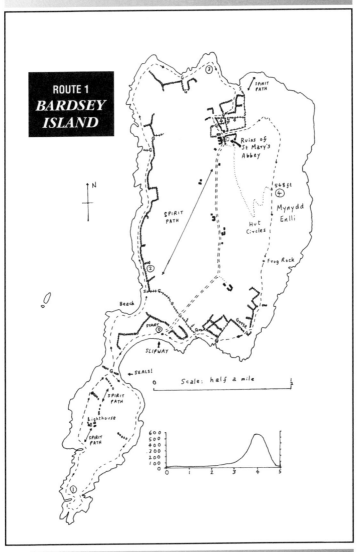

ROUTE 1
BARDSEY ISLAND

Distance:	4¼ miles
Start:	Caergwrle railway station, grid ref.: SJ 309573
OS Maps:	Pathfinder 789 (Wrexham North), Explorer 256, Landranger 117 (Chester)
Public Transport:	Trains run to Caergwrle from Wrexham and Bidston (tel. 0345 484950) Buses include no. 26 (Wrexham - Mold, tel. 01978 266166)

Introduction

Alfred Watkins wrote in Chapter XXIII of *The Old Straight Track* how Hermes becomes 'the leader over unknown trackways of departed souls to the nether world'. This link between paths and the dead is strengthened by research in Germany by Ulrich Magin and quoted by Paul Devereux in *Symbolic Landscapes*. Magin wrote of special corpse roads leading to cemeteries, running in straight lines and known as ghost paths. Devereux goes on to cite examples of straight spirit paths from all corners of the world. They are also associated with the spirit journeys of the shamans or enlightened ones during the temporary 'death' of a trance state.

The highlight of this walk is a Corpse Road recorded by R.J.A. Dutton in *Hidden Highways of North Wales*. Its northern terminus is in the area of the monastery of Hawarden (SJ305662). Going south towards the cemetery at Gresford (SJ345549), the line goes through a crossroads on the eastern edge of Llay (a good name for a place visited by a ley!) at SJ33955590. A Methodist chapel is marked here on the 1900 OS map. Follow a dead straight (!) section of this Corpse Road for half a mile between SJ32855875 and SJ33155810.

Route

(Mile 0) Walk downhill from the railway station, turn right to pass under a railway bridge and go ahead to cross a bridge over the Afon Alun. Bear left, passing Rhyddyn Hill on your right. Just before you reach Fellows Lane on your left, turn right up the access drive for

Rhyddyn Farm. Look for a waymarked stile on your right, turn right to cross it, then turn left to climb towards another stile. Notice a row of trees away to your left, at the back of the farm. These mark the line of Wat's Dyke. (This earthwork ran along the northern part of the border between the English and the Welsh. Its better engineering

The Corpse Road, east of Caergwrle

and siting may reflect a slightly later date than the late eighth century Offa's Dyke.)

Go ahead over the stile and walk with woodland behind an old wall on your right. Trees now clothe the slopes of Bryn-y-gaer's ancient hillfort (Caer Estyn). Cross over another stile at the highest point and cast your eye over the village of Hope, with its church, away to your left. Continue downhill and bear left to reach a stile giving access to the B5373 road where it is joined by an access road coming from a quarry on your right. Go right along the B5373 for 10 yards before taking a stile beside a gate on your left. Bear right along the signposted path down to a stone stile and maintain this direction to reach another signpost beside a gate at the corner of a lane. Leaving this on your right, go ahead over a stile and pass a hedge and buildings on your right. Continue down a slope to a damp meadow where there may be a pond on your right. Reach the far corner to go ahead over a stile **(Mile 1)** and pass Silverdale on your right.

You are now following the route of an old packhorse trail between Corwen and Chester, as so lovingly described in R.J.A. Dutton's book *Hidden Highways of North Wales*. Take the gate into the field ahead and continue through three more fields to reach a road opposite Shordley Hall. Turn right along this road and look out for a stile beside a gate on your left. Turn left to cross this and follow the left-hand side of a field. Continue over two stiles in rapid succession, bear left to a fieldgate near trees and go ahead with the hedge on your left in the next field. Notice a small footbridge on your left and stop in the corner of this field. Do not take the gate ahead!

Turn right to walk along the Corpse Road, keeping the hedge on your left in the first two fields **(Mile 2)**. Cross a footbridge and walk with a hedge on your right in the third field. Reach a prominent oak tree at the next corner. Go ahead to reach a gate which gives access to Cobblers Lane. This is an old drovers' road which earned its name because of the cobbles (now under its metalled surface) placed along it to give a better grip for draught animals pulling heavy carts to Ffrwd Ironworks in the 17th century. Turn right along Cobblers Lane and notice the access lane for a house on your right. The fields on your left here were used for the dyeing of cloth in the 12th century, being called Blue Field, Red Field and White Field, as R.J.A. Dutton observes in his excellent book. Continue along Cobblers Lane, passing Dark Lane on your left and bearing left at the next fork **(Mile 3)**.

St Mary's Abbey, Bardsey Island (Route 1)

Viewpoint from the promenade beside the River Usk, Brecon (Route 14)

A June sunset seen from the 1138ft summit of Carn Ingli (Route 12)

The reclining angel profile of Carn Ingli seen from the east (Route 12)

Go ahead at a crossroads with the B5373 to follow Rhyddyn Hill back down to the Afon Alun **(Mile 4)**. Bear left to retrace your steps across the bridge over the river and return to Caergwrle railway station.

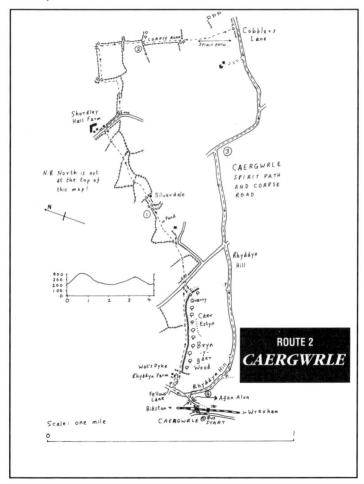

Distance:	8¾ miles
Start:	Dudley Armss Hotel, Llandrillo, grid ref.: SJ 034371 Explorer 255 (Llangollen and Berwyn),Landranger 125 (Bala)
Public Transport:	Bus no. 94 Barmouth - Dolgellau - Wrexham, tel. 01248 750444

Introduction

Moel Ty-uchaf is a well-preserved circle of 41 low stones which are spaced closely together, except for two wide gaps. It enjoys a superb location, overlooking the Dee valley from an altitude of 1450ft in the Berwyn Mountains.

Mathematicians have a field-day here. Robin Heath diverts to this place in his highly-recommended book *A Key to Stonehenge*. Following in the footsteps of Professor Alexander Thom, he shows how our ancestors used their technology to work out the relationships between the sun, moon and earth. Heath found Eclipse year/Solar year and Lunar year/Solar year ratios built into this megalithic monument.

George Terence Meaden offers a different reason for the creation of this ring of stones in his book *The Goddess of the Stones*. Meaden's theory compares interestingly with a dream recorded by your author on Carn Ingli in which the goddess showed what stone circles are. The goddess, in this case taken to be Rhiannon, held her hands in the form of a cup. This became a cross-section of the earth, with the soil a vivid orange and the goddess' fingers a brilliant white. White lines went out in all directions from these cupped fingers. Above was the beautiful symmetry of a dome over the cup. This was a more subtle, heavenly, structure. Within the domed cup or cauldron was a whirling vortex of brilliant white energy. There seemed to be an exchange from above and below, between heaven and earth. This white energy or spirit was being channelled along the white lines running through the orange earth. The vision then zoomed in for a close-up of the tips of the goddess' fingers. These formed the standing stones of a stone circle.

Dispute the reasons for this structure and the special nature of its site, but recognise that it does stand demanding an explanation. The Dragon Project monitored for radiation here between 1979 and 1983 (your author was one of Paul Devereux's volunteers). No exceptional results were found in 1983, although there were high readings in 1982, as reported by Paul Devereux's book *Places of Power*. The Dragon Project was attracted to Moel Ty-uchaf by an event in 1974. Keith Critchlow, who recorded his impressions in

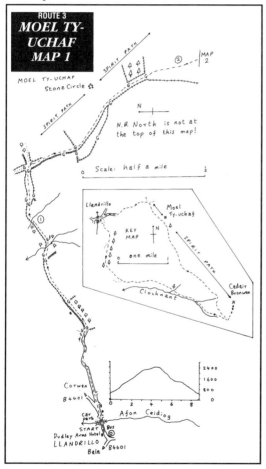

ROUTE 3
MOEL TY-UCHAF MAP 1

MOEL TY-UCHAF
Stone Circle

SPIRIT PATH

SPIRIT PATH

MAP 2

②

N.B. North is not at the top of this map!

N

Scale: half a mile

Llandrillo

Moel Ty-uchaf

KEY MAP

N

one mile

Clochnant

Cadair Bronwen

SPIRIT PATH

2400
1600
800
0

0 2 4 6 8

Cotwen
B4401

Afon Ceidiog

Car park

START
Dudley Arms Hotel
LLANDRILLO
Bala B4401

Bus

his book *Time Stands Still*, happened to be here in January 1974, when there was an earth tremor. Strange 'earthlights' were also observed.

Leys have long been associated with UFOs. Tony Wedd was a

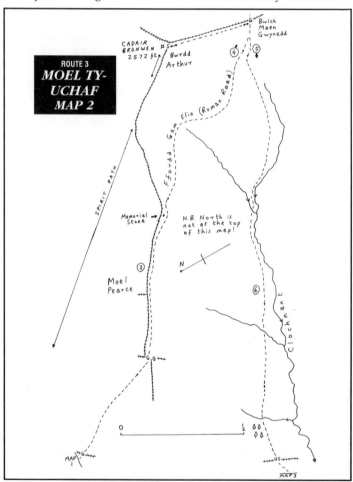

famous ley hunter who recognised leys or spirit paths as 'magnetic currents' used by 'flying saucers'. This idea worked well with the thoughts of Frenchman Aimé Michel, whose book *Flying Saucers and the Straight Line Mystery* appeared in 1958. Paul Devereux tackled the question of UFOs in his books *Earthlights* (1982) and *Earth Lights Revelation* (1989). In 1999 a book by Tony Dodd, Britain's leading UFO detective, entitled *Alien Investigator*, appeared to remind me of a strange story about the 'earth tremor' at Moel Ty-uchaf on January 23, 1974. I had heard such tales from locals who knew key witnesses but hadn't wanted to become associated with such unlikely things as 'flying saucers' (it's enough to be pointed out as a ley hunter). It would be negligent to fail to record, however, that local witnesses discount the idea of an earthquake that night. They speak of an explosion, the

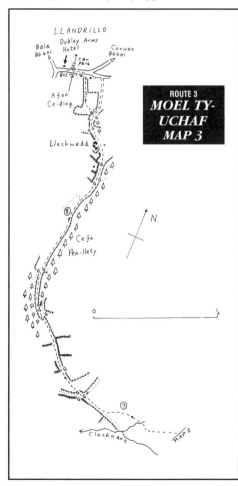

ROUTE 3
**MOEL TY-UCHAF
MAP 3**

discovery of a 'flying saucer' and of bodies of aliens being taken in boxes from the village of Llandderfel to Porton Down by the army. Large numbers of military vehicles were seen in the area for weeks after the incident.

Many leys or spirit paths converge or radiate from Moel Ty-uchaf. My dowsing rods suggested that the most important ran through a stone just outside the circle on its western side, through the circle and in the direction of Castell Dinas Bran at an angle of 72 degrees (76 minus 4 for magnetic variation). The next, which became the object of this walk, ran at an angle of 319 degrees (323-4) to a cairn on the 2572ft summit of Cadair Bronwen. Is this mountain seen as the breast of the goddess Branwen? With Rhiannon and Arianrhod, Branwen is one of the three Matriarchs of Britain. A provider of plenty who endures suffering, Branwen's story appears in the Second Branch of the Mabinogi. The plateau at this mountain summit is known as Bwrdd Arthur and is a contender for King Arthur's Round Table.

Route
(Mile 0) Face the Dudley Arms Hotel and go right to cross the bridge over the Afon Ceidiog. Pass the village hall and war memorial cross, then fork right up a no-through road, towards the afforested hills.

At the end of the metalled lane, ignore a waymarked stile on your left. Take the gate ahead and bear left with a track which affords a fine view over the Dee valley on your left. Keep above woodland on your left, ford a stream and take a gate ahead. Follow the track across another stream **(Mile 1)** and go through another gate ahead to reach a cross-tracks where a sign warns you to 'keep on the road'.

Turn right along the uphill track. The stone circle of Moel Ty-uchaf is above on your left, before the track reaches a plantation of conifer trees on your left. Continue past this plantation **(Mile 2)**. Go ahead along the track and **(Mile 3)** reach an inscribed stone on your left. This states 'Carnedd John Fronllan, Llangwm, 1891' and is a monument to a drover who was caught here in bad weather and died. A path bears right around the peak of Cadair Bronwen on your left and reaches **(Mile 4)** the pass Bwlch Maen Gwynedd. Don't go ahead through the small metal, waymarked gate!

Turn left to walk uphill beside a fence on your right to the summit of Cadair Bronwen (set on Bwrdd Arthur). Retrace your steps down to the small, metal, waymarked gate and turn right. Soon fork left down the valley, keeping above the stream on your left **(Mile 5)**.

(Mile 6) Aim for a plantation of conifer trees and pass these on your right. Continue over a stile to the left of a gate ahead. **(Mile 7)** Converge with the track coming up sharply from a ford on your left.

When a track descends from the hillside on your right, go ahead through the gate in the corner beside which is a bridlepath signpost. Almost immediately, bear right through a gate to take a grassy track. Descend through forest **(Mile 8)**. When the track forks left down to a hairpin bend, bear right with the forest's perimeter fence on your right.

Descend to the buildings of Llechwedd. Leave Llechwedd's metalled access lane to bear left over a waymarked stile. Cross a field to a stile in the far corner and take this to follow an enclosed path past the side of the village hall on your right to return to the road in Llandrillo. Go left to retrace your steps to the bridge and the bus stops near the Dudley Arms Hotel.

ROUTE 4
LLYNNAU CREGENNEN

Distance:	12½ miles
Start:	Llwyngwril railway station, grid ref.: SH 589097
Finish:	Eldon Square, Dolgellau, grid ref.: SH 728178
OS Maps:	Outdoor Leisure 23 (Snowdonia - Cadair Idris), Landranger 124 (Dolgellau)
Public Transport:	Trains run to Llwyngwril from Machynlleth and Pwllheli (tel. 0345 484950). Bus no.28 (Tywyn-Llwyngwril-Dolgellau, tel. 01248 750444) links the two ends of this walk.
Accommodation:	Kings youth hostel (tel. 01341 422392) is on this route (9½ miles from the start). There is a highly-recommended guesthouse and other holiday accommodation) near the start at Pentre Bach, Llwyngwril (tel. 01341 250294), run by Nick Smyth, who is a rambler, a ley hunter and has dreamt with the author on Carn Ingli.

Introduction

Modern tourists worship the beauty of nature at these lakes on a plateau overshadowed by Tyrrau Mawr and offering splendid views over the Mawddach estuary and Barmouth. The spirit seems to move people here, with the Quakers suffering persecution in this area in the 17th century.

This walk follows a spirit path which pierces a complex of ancient monuments like a lance going through a ring. The area had fascinated me for years, led me to dream there and shown me a confusing pattern of leys before I stepped back from the intensity of its centre and, by chance, found myself keeping my daughter Michelle amused on a walk above Llwyngwril by dowsing at a stone row known as the Waun Oer Stones (grid ref. SH 617113). Stone rows are rare in Wales (unlike Dartmoor) so it is impressive, even with just three stones still standing, two more recumbent and three supposed missing. Its real impact didn't dawn on me until after the walk when I drew the line I had dowsed with my daughter on the map. At an angle of 60 degrees (64-4 for magnetic variation) this equates to the moonrise in its northerly minor standstill, or approximates to the Beltane (early May) and Lugnasadh (early August) sunrises – the famous Dragon Line from Cornwall to Norfolk described by Hamish Miller and Paul Broadhurst in *The Sun and the Serpent* runs at an angle of 63 degrees. The line drawn on my map linked this stone row with a cairn at SH 604105 and a standing stone at SH 601103 to the west and with a cairn and a standing stone at SH 662138 in the east. This is the westernmost of the two standing stones known as the Bryn Seward Stones. Not on my spirit path, but within one mile to the east at SH 634115, is a

The stone row above Llwyngwril

cairn known as Bedd y Brenin (Grave of the King).

Continuing eastwards along the line I had dowsed, the spirit path goes through a prominent standing stone near the ancient track known as the Ffordd Ddu (Black Road) at SH 652133. It passes close to another standing stone at SH 662138 and the Arthog stone circle at SH 653139 is a quarter of a mile to the north of the line. This ruined ring has an egg-shape with all the characteristics proposed by Professor Thom, plus two extra stones at its east end (perhaps moved when the monument was incorporated into a field-wall) and a white quartz boulder which gave me a mild electric shock. The

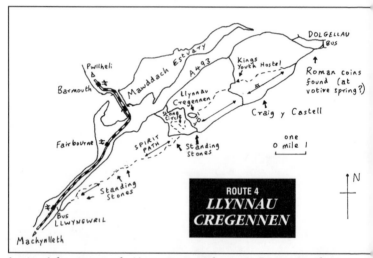

ROUTE 4
LLYNNAU CREGENNEN

basis of the ring is a half-size 3,4,5, right angled triangle. The arcs have radii of 2, 4.5 and 3 megalithic yards and the perimeter has a value of 8.14 megalithic rods. My dowsing suggests a link with Bardsey Island, which is visible on clear days. This stone circle is near the site of Llys Bradwen (Bradwen's Court). In my ignorance I presumed this to be a reference to Branwen and when I came to dream here I expected to feel the femininity of the place. On the contrary, it proved to be stridently masculine and I have since read that Bradwen was a local (male) ruler. He is said to have lived in the

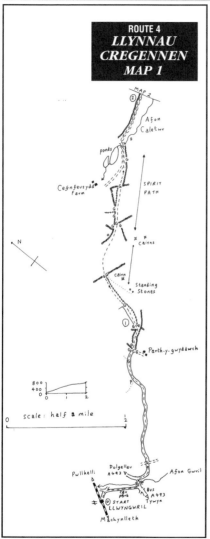

ROUTE 4
LLYNNAU CREGENNEN MAP 1

MAP 2

Afon Caletwr

ponds

Cefnfeusydd Farm

SPIRIT PATH

Cairns

Cairn

Standing Stones

Parth-y-gwyddwch

800
400
0
0   1   2

scale: half a mile

0   1/2

Pwllheli   Dolgellau
A493   Afon Gwril

Bus

car park   A493
START   Tywyn
LLWYNGWRIL

Machynlleth

Middle Ages, although Roman pottery has been found on the site of his court. I've also come across the name Bradwen in South Wales, so there may be more to this. In Glamorgan the Maen Bradwen or Carreg Bica standing stone near Neath (SS 725995) is said to bathe in the Afon Nedd every Easter Sunday morning.

If you have time, do make a diversion up Pared y cefn-hir, where there was a hillfort on its pencil-thin ridge at a height of 1200ft (your reward for the steep climb is the most magnificent view over the Mawddach). The spirit path continues eastwards by glancing the southern side of Craig y Castell (SH 694158) and reaching the centre of Dolgellau by way of the site where Roman coins were found in 1695. These are thought to have been votive offerings in sacred springs.

Route
(Mile 0) Take the access lane from the station to the centre of Llwyngwril and turn left across a bridge.

Face the Garthangharad Inn and go right up Ffordd y Coleg. Soon bear left uphill away from the river. Follow the metalled lane, keeping above the sea on your left, until it turns right through a gate to serve the farm of Parth-y-gwyddwch.

Go ahead along a walled, grassy track **(Mile 1)**, still overlooking the sea on your left. Converge with a lane ascending sharply from your left and pass a pond. Cross a concrete bridge over the Afon Caletwr. Go ahead with the lane **(Mile 2)** and pass the stone row of three standing stones known as the Waun Oer Stones on your left (the owner allows access to these stones, but not for dogs). Pass the two Bryn Seward Stones **(Mile 3)**.

Follow the lane through a forestry plantation and reach a signposted junction. Bear right here to climb with a path through the forest. Continue over a stile in a fence ahead, cross a stream, take a gate in a wall ahead and climb to converge with the firm track of the Ffordd Ddu **(Mile 4)**.

Go left along the Ffordd Ddu. Go ahead through one gate but do not take the next gate, giving access to a walled

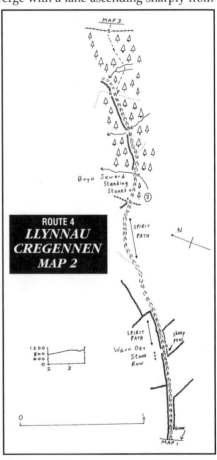

ROUTE 4
*LLYNNAU
CREGENNEN
MAP 2*

descending lane. Go right at this corner to continue with a wall on your left. Pass a standing stone which marks the spirit path on your left before meeting a road **(Mile 5)**.

Go left along the road for just a few yards before bearing right off the road to take a gate in the wall on your right. Continue by bearing left to pass a farmhouse. Turn right over a clapper (flat stone slab) bridge across the Afon Arthog and reach the site of Llys Bradwen (Bradwen's Court). Bear left to a gate **(Mile 6)** and follow a walled path a short distance, then turn right to walk with a wall on your right. Look over it after passing through the second gate ahead to see the stone circle.

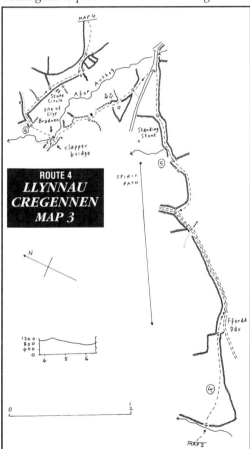

Continue to the corner ahead and bear left uphill, as signposted. Walking with a wall on your left, come to a stone stile in the corner ahead, cross this and bear left to the road near the bigger lake of Llynnau Cregennen, with the distinctive peak of Pared y cefn-hir on your left ahead. Turn right away from it to follow the road. Pass a rock marking boggy ground which makes a compass needle swing violently to your left **(Mile 7)**. Before the road comes to a junction preceded by a gate in a wall across it, turn left to pass a standing stone which is near the spirit path. Continue past the smaller lake on your right, then turn left to pass the bigger lake on your left and reach the path running along the foot of Pared y cefn-hir. Turn right along this, soon being joined by a wall on your right **(Mile 8)**.

Bear left at a corner to go ahead through a gate and turn right to go through another gate and bear left, leaving Ty'n Llidiart on your right. Walk with a wall on your right through four fields, then with a stream on your right. Reach a lane which comes over a bridge across this **(Mile 9)** and go ahead until this bends left. Go ahead along a

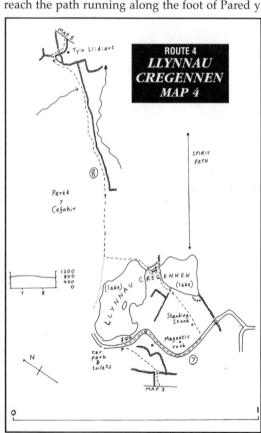

ROUTE 4
LLYNNAU CREGENNEN
MAP 4

waymarked woodland path to another bend in the lane and descend to Kings youth hostel.

Go right along the lane from the youth hostel, soon crossing a

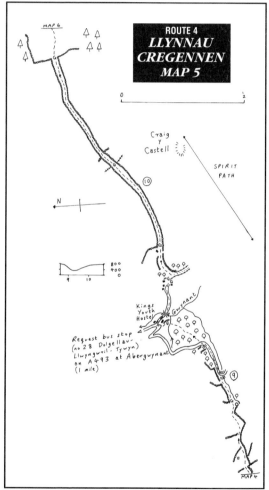

bridge over Gwynant. Continue to the end of the metalled lane, then bear right through the higher of two gates. Almost immediately, turn sharply left and climb to join a walled, grassy track **(Mile 10)**. Emerge from this to walk with another forestry plantation behind a wall on your left and descend to take a gate and bear left to join the access road for Gelliwyd Fawr **(Mile 11)**.

Go right along the road, keep left when a road comes in sharply from your right at a junction, descend to Dolgellau and bear right **(Mile 12)**. Ffordd Cader leads to Eldon Square, where buses stop, and there is a Snowdonia National Park Visitors Centre in the centre of Dolgellau.

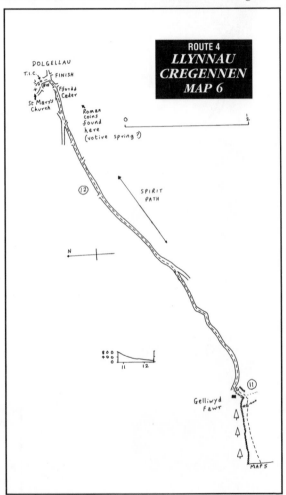

Looking south from Carn-Ingli to the Preselis over the goddess' breast and head (Route 12)

Moel Ty-uchaf stone circle (Route 3)

The western cairn, Drygarn Fawr (Route 9)

Distance:	5 miles
Start:	Broad Street, Montgomery, grid ref.: SO 222964
OS Maps:	Explorer 216 (Montgomery), Landranger 137 (Ludlow)
Public Transport:	Tel. 01597 826643 for details of bus services to Montgomery, including buses from Shrewsbury, Welshpool and Newtown

Introduction

Readers of the Turnstone Press edition (1983) of *The Ley Hunter's Manual* by Alfred Watkins will be familiar with the picture of St Nicholas's Church, Montgomery, on its front cover. Paul Devereux and Ian Thomson examined the ley running through Montgomery in their book *The Ley Hunter's Companion*. This circular walk takes in part of that ley. Devereux and Thomson found seven significant points along a line running for less than six miles. There are probably other lines converging on what has been a site of strategic importance since at least the Iron Age. This is the sort of border town where time stands still and it feels as if you are stepping into the pages of Phil Rickman's novel *Crybbe*.

The ley, or spirit path, starts from an old crossways in Offa's Dyke at grid ref. SO 25839130. This walk joins the ley as it approaches the B4385 road, with which it coincides for half a mile. Going north at an angle of 326 degrees, this stretch of road can be seen to align with the church and castle in Montgomery. Passing close to the Robber's Grave in the churchyard, it passes an old standing stone (marking the ley?) near the foot of Arthur Street (grid ref. SO 22279669, between the church and the castle).

The castle occupies the mighty rock above the town. Begun in 1223, it is near an ancient earthwork. I dowsed the ley going through the ruins of the Well Tower. Look back from the castle keep over the church and along the road which marks the ley as it runs south-

south-eastwards to Offa's Dyke. Devereux and Thomson detail the ley extending north-north-west by way of Hen Domen (SO 21369802) and a Roman fort at SO 20809890, built on a prehistoric site.

The proximity of the spirit path to the Robber's Grave is intriguing. On April 20, 1821, John Davies was accused by William

Jones of assaulting him and stealing his watch worth 30 shillings and five pence in coppers on the road between Welshpool and Newtown the previous night. Highway robbery was punishable by death, so when Davies was found guilty by a jury, he was executed at Montgomery on Thursday, September 6, 1821. Davies swore that he was innocent and prayed that the grass would not grow on his grave for a generation, as a sign from God of his innocence. As Davies declared his innocence before swinging from the rope, there was a tremendous thunderstorm. The execution would have

Montgomery Castle

probably taken place outside the old gaol building passed on your left as you climb the steep lane to the castle from the back of the town hall. The body was buried in a part of the churchyard that had not yet been consecrated, on the north side of the church, where it was traditional to play games. This may be a reminder of pagan

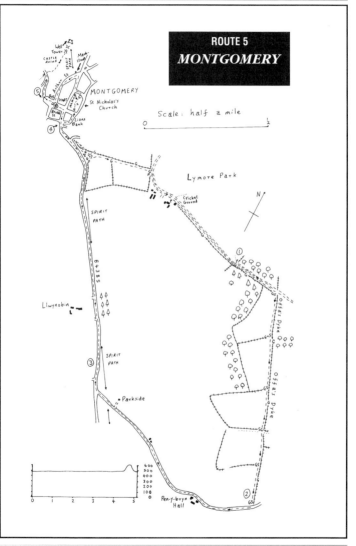

ROUTE 5
MONTGOMERY

Scale: half a mile

Lymore Park

SPIRIT PATH

B4385

Llwynobin

SPIRIT PATH

Parkside

Pen-y-bryn Hall

MONTGOMERY

St Nicholas's Church

Lions Bank

Castle Ruins

Cricket Ground

Offa's Dyke

associations. It is recorded that no grass would grow on the grave for the required generation, while a bare patch in the form of a cross could still be seen this century. Local tradition is that Davies was 'planted' with the evidence and 'set up' by a rival in love, so this may be an example of the power of the spirit to affect the growth of grass. A much longer-lasting example of this phenomenon is the bare patch on Dragon Hill, Uffington (Oxfordshire), where St George slew the dragon. I dowsed the primary ley from the Robber's Grave as going eastwards to Corndon Hill.

Route
(Mile 0) With the town hall and its clock tower behind you, go down Broad Street, passing the Checkers Hotel on your left. Turn right along Bishop's Castle Street. Pass The Crown on your right. Follow the road as it curves to the left and descends. Immediately after the children's playground on your left, go left to cross a stile and turn right to walk with a football field on your left and a fence on your right. Turn right to cross another stile in this fence and immediately turn left, as waymarked by a yellow arrow, to walk with the fence on your left. Continue through a small wooden gate and across a footbridge. Turn left to walk along the left-hand edge of a field. Continue along the left-hand edge of a second field.

Turn right along a metalled track which is waymarked as a public bridleway with a blue arrow. Ignore an access track going to a house on your right, pass a cricket ground on your left and go ahead to reach a cattle grid **(Mile 1)**.

Continue over the cattle grid and along the metalled track through woodland. Do not proceed over another cattle grid when the woodland ends. Turn right along the Offa's Dyke Path, which is waymarked with an acorn symbol. Walk with Offa's Dyke surmounted by a hedge on your left.

(Mile 2) Emerge on a lane. Don't continue southwards along the Offa's Dyke Path. Turn right along this lane and pass Pen-y-bryn Hall on your left. Look out for the drive up to Parkside on your right, go ahead about 15 yards to where trees shade the lane and dowse for the spirit path to Montgomery Castle which crosses the lane here at an angle of about 326 degrees (330-4 for magnetic variation). Continue to the B4385 road **(Mile 3)**.

Turn right along the B4385 road. The ley converges with it when Llwynobin is on your left and there is woodland on your right. The road now coincides with the ley and the tower of St Nicholas's Church, Montgomery, appears straight ahead, with Montgomery Castle beyond it. Follow the road into Montgomery.

(Mile 4) Pass Tan-y-mur on your right but do turn right shortly afterwards up Lions Bank. Bear left to pass a house built on the site of the old town ditch in 1726 on your right. Turn left at Church Bank and take the gate into the churchyard on your right. Pass St Nicholas's Church on your right and approach the gate on the far side of the churchyard. About 15 yards before it, on your left, is a simple wooden cross and a rose bush marking the Robber's Grave.

Go ahead to leave the churchyard and turn left to Princes Street. Turn right down to a road junction where you turn sharply left up Arthur Street. Notice the markstone at the upper end of a row of terraced cottages on your right. Continue along Arthur Street to the town hall.

Turn right to take a lane at the back of the town hall which is signposted as being for the castle. After a steep climb, reach the castle car park on your right and go right along the access path to the castle.

Retrace your steps from the castle to the back of the town hall **(Mile 5)** and go ahead to Broad Street.

Distance:	3 miles
Start:	Ysbyty Cynfyn church, grid ref.: SN 753791
OS Maps:	Explorer 213 (Devil's Bridge), Landranger 135 (Aberystwyth)
Public Transport:	There is a postbus (no. 596) from Aberystwyth to Ysbyty Cynfyn, otherwise walk 1½ miles south from the bus stop in Ponterwyd served by bus no. 501 from Aberystwyth. The express coach between Aberystwyth and Birmingham (no. 522) also stops in Ponterwyd. Tel. 01545 572504 for details of all bus services. There is a seasonal train service from Aberystwyth to Devil's Bridge (two miles south of Ysbyty Cynfyn). Tel. 01970 625819 for Vale of Rheidol Railway information.

Introduction

This is a marvellous walk around wild, rugged country, overlooking the gorge of the Rheidol, with its beautiful waterfalls. The earth energies seem to come from very deep here. The five large standing stones set in the churchyard wall of the church of St John at Ysbyty Cynfyn suggest that this Christian site evolved from a pagan stone circle. Sacred site continuity is common. The relatively easy transfer from Druid to Celtic Christian spirituality in Wales (based on direct links between Ancient Britons, the Jews, and early Christians and, indeed, the family of Jesus - read *Bloodline of the Holy Grail* by Laurence Gardner, *Celt, Druid and Culdee* by Isabel Elder, *The Drama of the Lost Disciples* by George Jowett, *The Coming of the Saints* by John Taylor, *Did Our Lord Visit Britain?* by Rev. C.C. Dobson, *The Legendary XII Hides of Glastonbury* by Ray Gibbs and *The Glastonbury Zodiac* by Mary Caine) meant that it was natural for worship to continue at time-honoured sites. Even in the land lost to the Saxons, where St Augustine was sent as a missionary from Rome (and how many English Christians assume that the coming of St Augustine to Kent in 597 was the start of Christianity in this country?) there is evidence in the letter of 601 from Pope Gregory to Abbot Mellitus, who was made Archbishop of London to convert the English, that the 'heathen's' temples were converted into churches. Winchester Cathedral is said to have been built on a stone circle, while St Paul's Cathedral (so intriguingly used for the marriage of Prince Charles with Princess Diana, when royal weddings usually take place in

An ancient stone circle above Ysbyty Cynfyn

Westminster Abbey) stands on the site of the Temple of .... Diana! This helps to explain why spirit paths are linked with prehistoric sacred sites and Christian churches. The existence of coffin trails or corpse roads brings more involvement with churches and cemeteries. Even post-Reformation chapels seem to have been placed on traditional sacred sites (often at crossroads). The Templars and the Cistercians seem to have known some secret knowledge in the Middle Ages. They are both connected with this place. The church was used as a hospice for pilgrims travelling to Strata Florida Abbey (Ysbyty Cynfyn is Welsh for 'first boundary hospital'). The Templars worked a leadmine in the hillside on the northern side of the river.

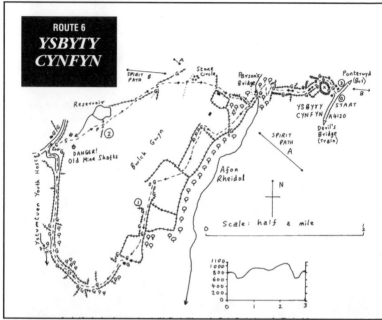

Spend time in the churchyard to find a grave under a tree and next to the railings on the left of the church's porch. The grave is that of Isaac Hughes, who died on 6th March, 1856, aged 32 and of his son Hugh, who died on 1st March, his daughter Hannah, who died on 10th March, aged 3, and of the first recorded quadruplets, Margaret, Elizabeth, Catherine and Isaac, who all died within six days of their birth on February 17th, 1856. Only their mother, Margaret, survived that year's outbreak of typhoid.

George Borrow came this way and was urged to see 'Pont yr Offeiriad, or the Parson's Bridge, because in the old time the clergyman passed over it every Sunday to do duty in the church here'. Rev. Richard Davies was known to use it in 1722 as a short cut when officiating on the same day at both Ysbyty Cynfyn and Ystumtuen. Until 1951, the bridge was just a plank hung from the sides of the gorge by chains above the Rheidol, which is a deep-cutting river. The steep slopes of its valley sides have saved the native sessile oak trees from being sacrificed to the ploughman.

The ancient stone circle on the hillside across the river to the west of the church still resounded with spirit when I lay down in it one June evening. Known as the Bwlch Gwyn or Temple Cairn Circle, this small ellipse fits Thom's megalithic yard (2.72ft) when scaled down to one quarter of a megalithic yard. Then the distance between the foci of the ellipse is 2¾m/yds, which is exactly half of the long axis. The short axis is 4¾m/yds, while the perimeter is 16m/yds. This is exactly half the size of the ring Nine Stones (Winterbourne Abbas) in Dorset and both rings have their stones graded in height.

Dowsing revealed the most important spirit path (A) running through it to be the 310 degree line of the summer solstice sunset. A glance at the OS map reveals how tantalisingly close this comes to connecting with other sacred sites. Another spirit path (B) runs, at 93 degrees, very close to the equinox sunrise line, eastwards to Ysbyty Cynfyn church, while going westwards to glance the southern edge of Castell Bwa-drain (SN 713794) and reach the coast at the northern edge of the old hillfort on Pendinas (SN 584806).

Route

(Mile 0) Pass through the gate to the right of Ysbyty Cynfyn church. Follow the path around to the left, then ahead until you stand above a wooded valley. Go through the gate on your right to follow a path which zigzags down through the oak trees to a footbridge across the river. This is Parson's Bridge and the river is the Rheidol.

Cross the footbridge, turn left and keep the fence on your left as you go ahead across two stiles. Walk with the fence on your left around the edge of a field to a stile in its far right corner. Cross this stile, go ahead along a track, go ahead over another stile and bear right towards a ruin. Pass this on your right as you continue with a fence on your left **(Mile 1)**.

Cross a field to a gate giving access to a farmyard. Follow the clear track which bends until it meets a road. Go down to a junction with another road (which leads to Ystumtuen, where there was a youth hostel, on your left). Turn right to go uphill, reach a building on your left and bear right through a gate in the fence on your right. Climb to a stile which has lost its fence and be careful not to fall down old mine shafts! Climb to a reservoir ahead on your left **(Mile 2)**.

Cross a stile in a fence ahead and continue to take another stile in a fence coming up on your left. Keep the fence on your right until a stile ahead. Go over this and bear right down to the ancient stone circle. Pass this on your left as you descend to another stile. Go past a building on your right, take a stile into woodland ahead and keep descending. Switch a fence from your left to your right by going over another stile. Go down to rejoin your outward path, turn left, cross Parson's Bridge and retrace your steps back to Ysbyty Cynfyn **(Mile 3)**.

Distance:	2½ miles
Start:	Strata Florida car park, grid ref.: SN 746657 (or bus stop in Pontrhydfendigaid, grid ref.: SN 730664)
OS Maps:	Explorer 187, Landranger 135 (Aberystwyth)
Public Transport:	Buses nos. 561 & 562 run to Pontrhydfendigaid from Aberystwyth, no. 588 comes from Lampeter (tel. 01545 572504)

Introduction

This is one of the most hallowed spots in Wales. The Cistercians built an abbey here in the 12th century. They re-located after first settling at what is now known as Yr hen Fynachlog (the old monastery) two miles to the west at SN 718646. This is near the Afon Fflur, hence the beautiful name, meaning 'Way of Flowers'. Perhaps they knew to come to this sacred region but the locals didn't advise them of the exact spot until trust had been gained. The Abbey of the Blessed Virgin Mary became the place of burial for the Princes of Deheubarth (Dyfed), while in 1238 there was an assembly of Welsh princes to swear allegiance to Llywelyn Fawr of Gwynedd's son, Dafydd. This was an important place and graveyard much earlier than that. Look behind the relatively modern church dedicated to St Mary in the cemetery next to the abbey ruins. Leaning outside its eastern wall is a stone carved with a cross and dated to between AD 500 and 750. This is proof of a sacred site here in the Golden Age of the Celtic saints (see page 184 of *The Cistercian Abbey of Strata Florida* by S.W. Williams, 1889). There was also a prehistoric hillfort to the north at Pen y Bannau, overlooking Strata Florida.

A local author going under the pen-name of Llowarch wrote about a ley running between Strata Florida and Llanilar church (SN 624751) in his 'Weird Wonders of Wales' column in *The Cambrian News* (6th November, 1987). Earlier that year he had described this alignment in *The Ley Hunter* no. 103. At about 307 degrees, this isn't too far short of the summer solstice sunset line. It passes to the northern side of a motte (mound) at SN 718678, the hillside occupied by Ystrad Meurig hillfort (not the Norman castle) at SN 708687 (where there seems to be a notch on the skyline), glances the northern edge of Pen-y-castell (SN 630746) and Llanilar church would then seem to be its last significant point. This doesn't give a satisfying end at the coast which would fit in with local legend that a secret passage runs between Strata Florida and the sea, specifically the Monk's Cave or Twll Twrw at SN 555744 (which is on a line from Strata Florida of about 293 degrees, connected, perhaps, with the sunset at Beltane and Lugnasadh in early May and early August).

The mysterious pit in the centre of Strata Florida Abbey

Dowsing for my own leys, I found the most important (and the spirit path marked on my map) runs at an angle of 320 degrees from the high altar, through the yew tree associated with Dafydd ap Gwilym, over the grave of the Unknown Tramp and without any further points of significance on the map. The distance between the high altar and the yew tree (also visited by Llowarch's ley) is negligible, so we virtually share the same line. It seemed appropriate that my spirit path should be linked with the moon, however (moonset in northerly major standstill). Another spirit path was also dowsed from the curious hole in the centre of the abbey to the same yew tree, while a third ran from what seemed to be the base of the central pillar in the nave also to the yew tree. That yew tree has great significance.

The yew tree stands in the graveyard on the northern side of the abbey ruins. Dafydd ap Gwilym, Wales' greatest medieval poet, is said to be buried under it. This is highly unlikely as the tree is at least one thousand years old and the poet died around 1380. A rival bard, Gruffydd Gryg (from Anglesey) wrote about Dafydd ap Gwilym being buried beneath this yew tree whilst he was still alive. When Leland visited the abbey in 1536, there were 39 yew trees - more evidence for the ancient sanctity of this site. Anyway, George Borrow (whose *Wild Wales* was published in 1862) said a short poem to this tree when passing this way in 1854:

'O tree of yew, which here I spy,
By Ystrad Fflur's blest monast'ry,
Beneath thee lies, by cold Death bound,
The tongue for sweetness once renown'd.'

Dafydd ap Gwilym's own poetry rests more easily on the ear. When rebuked once by a friar for confessing his love for a maiden, Dafydd retorted:

'God is not cruel as old men say,
He will not damn us, though others may,
For the love we bear towards woman or maid ....,
Save only three, all the human race
Are born of a woman, in every place.'

The ley or spirit path was also dowsed going over the grave of the unknown tramp. This tramp died a pauper in the snow while walking towards Rhayader in 1929. He was buried like a prince at Strata Florida. His epitaph, composed by poet Evan Jenkins, reads:

'He died upon the hillside drear,
Alone where snow was deep,
By strangers he was carried here,
Where princes also sleep.'

Not far from the yew tree is another curious grave. Buried here on June 18th, 1756 is the leg of Henry Hughes Cooper. It was severed in a stage coach crash, but he later emigrated to the USA!

The strangest thing about the abbey is the pit at the crossing of the church. It is not aligned with the rest of the building and gives the feeling of pre-dating it. About three feet deep, stonelined and rectangular, it has steps leading down at both ends. The best theory is that it was some sort of baptism font. The noviciate monks may have passed through water in it to become full members of the brotherhood. If this is so, why don't other Cistercian houses have such a pit? Why is it placed both off-centre at the crossing and out of alignment?

Llowarch has written of a ghost-watch at the abbey at Christmas Eve, 1984, when a 'white shape' was seen. There is an old folktale of candles burning amid the ruins of Strata Florida and of a ghost of one of the monks seen rebuilding the altar at Christmas Eve. This may be the Mad Monk, whom tradition states was involved in forgery and died unrepentant. He is buried on a hillside well away from consecrated ground. A couple of years later, Llowarch returned to keep watch at Old Christmas Eve, allowing for the change in the calendar (which explains why the Orangemen march on 12th July to commemorate the Battle of the Boyne which was fought on 1st July, 1690, before the calendar was changed in this country). One of the party lost consciousness having put their hands into a small hole and Llowarch wonders if this was where the Holy Grail was hidden. The (thin) story both here and at Glastonbury is that the Holy Grail was brought from Glastonbury Abbey to Strata Florida Abbey by three monks at the Dissolution.

Here I touch upon a very deep and long story, part of which has been told in my booklet *Camlan - the true story?* and which, I trust, will form the basis of a novel intended to set the record straight as to what really happened at the end of the Arthurian period.

Dreams, psychic messages and compelling evidence for reincarnation mark this Quest. Suffice to say that the Holy Grail was taken from Chalice Well, Glastonbury, westwards for safe-keeping at Strata Florida by the full moon of the December after the Battle of Camlan, which was fought near Dinas Mawddwy on 23rd June (old calendar - 4th July modern calendar), probably in the year 537 (possibly 539). King Arthur was mortally wounded at Camlan and Glastonbury was now considered to be at risk from Saxon attack. The Holy Grail was moved in the sixth century, not the sixteenth.

Instead of three monks from Glastonbury Abbey, it was carried by three warrior saints. Presumably these became known as Sir Galahad, Sir Perceval and Sir Bors, the three knights who achieved the Grail Quest. Sabine Baring-Gould has concluded that St Cadoc was the original of Sir Galahad. Sir Pedrog seems to have been the original of Sir Perceval, while another knight who brought the Holy Grail to Strata Florida from Glastonbury was Derfel Gadarn of Camlan fame. Derfel was not Sir Bors, but his pupil. Sir Bors was probably the elderly Blaise and Derfel became his pupil when training to become the Merlin or Myrddin of Maelgwn Gwynedd (and eventually, in 570, to be buried on Bardsey Island, where he died as its third Abbot). Derfel carried the Holy Grail to safety without realising what it was. He stood in for Blaise. Psychic questing is too subjective to count as history so the story must be told in a novel.

However, this explains the complete lack of any reference to the Holy Grail in Glastonbury during the medieval period, when the monks of Glastonbury would have loved to have made money from owning it. I have checked this with Geoffrey Ashe and other experts at the Pendragon Society's annual meeting held in Glastonbury in 1998. It also explains the story of three monks taking the Holy Grail from Glastonbury to Strata Florida for safety. Why do this at the Dissolution, when Henry VIII's men were soon knocking at the door of Strata Florida Abbey in 1539? The Holy Grail was brought here one thousand years earlier.

As part of my personal Quest, I was directed to maintain a vigil for three nights in front of the high altar at Strata Florida Abbey at mid-winter. This was not to be a winter solstice, but the midpoint between November 1st 1996 and January 31st, 1997. I made these the nights of December 16th, 17th and (to consider the old calendar as well to complete the Druidical three) 27th (1996). The first night, I immediately became very tired (before 5pm, whilst there was still some daylight). Falling asleep, I dreamt that a lady (the guardian of the place?) came to see who I was and then welcomed me. I awoke within half an hour and I couldn't believe at first that she wasn't really sharing my sleeping-bag. I knew I had to light a candle, say a prayer and point a pentagram at the high altar at some point during the night, but not exactly when (I would 'know' when). Staying awake but relaxed, I lay in front of the high altar for hours. Then I suddenly 'knew' that I should light my candle, say my prayer and point my pentagram. As I completed this task, I turned around to witness the most magical sight of the (nearly full?) moon rising exactly in the doorway of the abbey's West End to shine through it upon me as I lay in front of the high altar. I felt blessed.

The second night was quiet, wet and misty. it seemed like a 'bridging' night. The third, on 27th December, was clear again and this time, as I faced the high altar and pointed my pentagram at the candle that I had lit earlier (then said my prayer), the moon (nearly new?) rose straight in front of me in the east. This was another magical moment which felt like a great blessing. No wonder that when I dowsed for spirit paths at Strata Florida, I found the most important to be 320 degrees (moonset in northerly major standstill).

A year later, after the publication of *Camlan - the true story?*, I was contacted by a lady who was able to send me some water from the Nanteos Cup and arrange for me to see this gnarled piece of olive wood which has such wonderful healing properties.

'Ah, blessed vision! blood of God!', wrote Tennyson.

The Nanteos Cup is, I believe, the Holy Grail that was kept hidden at Strata Florida. Guarded by the Steadmans after the Dissolution, then by the Powell family, it was kept at Nanteos House, near Aberystwyth (SN 620787). A replica still resides there. The real thing is kept at a secret location. Nanteos House is now a country house hotel and restaurant. The Holy Grail is the Cup used by Jesus at the Last Supper. It was brought to these shores by Joseph the Arimathea after the crucifixion.

Whilst seeing the Nanteos Cup, I was shown a book which contained startling information on Strata Florida, although something I had felt must be there. Read Chapter XII of *The Lost Magic of Christianity - Celtic Essene Connections* by Michael Poynder. This describes a landscape angel running north-south and touching Strata Florida in the west, its crowned goddess being at Craig Ty-crin (SN 775675). Pivoting this landscape angel to run west-east, its root chakra becomes the village of Pontrhydfendigaid (Bridge of the blessed ford) and Strata Florida Abbey is the solar plexus chakra. The crowned goddess fits the hilltop above Tyncwm. A 9½ mile walk around this area, including the Teifi Pools, is published in the

OS/Jarrold Pathfinder Guide *Mid Wales and the Marches Walks* by Laurence Main. Poynder's book also discloses that dowsing reveals how the mysterious pit could well have been a font fed by flowing water - as exceptional as the rest of this place.

My quest to find the holy well near Strata Florida to which Derfel Gadarn and company brought the Holy Grail from Glastonbury in December, 537, led me to plan to return there on Tuesday, 23 November, 1999, in order to try and find it with my dowsing rods in the forest to the south-east of the abbey ruins. Walking in that forest in October, 1999, I felt sure the well was somewhere in it. I

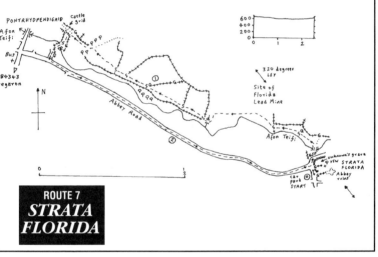

ROUTE 7
STRATA FLORIDA

vowed to return with a friend the next month and take my time to dowse for this well. My friend agreed to drive me there on Tuesday, 23 November, 1999. I had no idea where to search apart from a moonlit scene in a dream and trust in my dowsing rods. I was astonished to see a big colour picture in *The Guardian* of Monday, 22 November, 1999, of a mysterious holy well 'buried deep in forest in west Wales, on a hill above the ruined medieval Cistercian abbey of Strata Florida'. How strange that an obscure well should be pictured in colour in *The Guardian* on the very eve of our planned trip to dowse for such a site! Instead of dowsing for the well, I contacted the Forestry Commission, who revealed its location and asked that I keep this secret. As archaeologist Caroline Earwood remarked to me, 'You would never have found it in the dense forest'. Ms Earwood found the well by studying an aerial photograph. Please respect the need to keep this well's location a secret.

Route

(Mile 0) Visit the abbey ruins, then the adjacent cemetery (to see Dafydd ap Gwilym's yew tree, the Celtic Stone behind St Mary's Church, the grave of the severed leg and that of the unknown tramp). Go right to pass the cemetery and telephone box on your right. The road to Pontrhydfendigaid leads away to your left. As your road bears right, cross it to take a waymarked stile beside a gate ahead and follow the signposted path to a footbridge over the Afon Teifi. Cross this river and bear left. The route is waymarked and you keep the river on your left, passing the site of the Florida Lead Mine on your right. Cross a succession of stiles (the sixth is at **(Mile 1)**, where there is a small patch of woodland behind the fence on your left, between you and the river).

Join a track coming from your right. Maintain your direction along it, heading for the village of Pontrhydfendigaid. Reach a cattle grid and turn left over a stile. Continue across a footbridge and come to the road leading from Pontrhydfendigaid to Strata Florida Abbey (if starting from the bus stop, you will join this route here and leave it by turning right when returning to the bus stop). Go left along this road **(Mile 2)** to return to Strata Florida Abbey.

MAEN SERTH

Distance:	9 miles
Start:	St Winifred's Church, Llansantffraed-Cwmdeuddwr, grid ref.: SN 968677
OS Maps:	Explorer 200, Landranger 136 (Newtown) or 147 (Elan valley)
Public Transport:	There is a Royal Mail postbus from Llandrindod to the start of this walk, while buses running to Rhayader (just across the bridge from the start) include services from Llandrindod (the nearest railway station), Builth Wells (where there is also a railway station), Hereford, Aberystwyth, Newtown and Machynlleth (tel. 01597 826642).

Introduction

Cwmdeuddwr, the Valley of the Two Rivers, Wye and Elan, was the ritual centre of ancient Wales, according to John Michell and Christine Rhone *in Twelve-Tribe Nations and the Science of Enchanting the Landscape*. Leaving aside the issue of whether or not Wales had an identity in ancient times, this area is littered with ancient monuments, despite much of its area being flooded in modern times to give water to Birmingham.

St Winifred's is the modern name of the church at the start of this walk, but it was originally dedicated to St Bridget, or Bride, whose name comes from the Sanskrit *Braht* (the exalted one). A feast was traditionally held here every February, which was the time of the pagan feast of Imbolc, dedicated to Bride. Christianity is long-established here and the stone christening font in the church porch dates from the fifth century.

The high plateau west of Rhayader is splendid walking country. It is even possible to walk through remnants of the original sessile oak forest, while ancient monuments remind us of the great age of these paths. Maen Serth (Steep Stone) is a prominent standing stone which stands 7ft 2ins high, 6ins thick and 1ft 8ins broad, at an altitude of 1500ft. It was erected in the Bronze Age and had a cross carved on it around AD 800. The Welsh chieftain of Elvel, Einion Clud, was murdered by the English here after he had unhorsed Roger Mortimer in a tournament in the late 12th century.

Maen Serth

Maengwyngweddw (White-widow Stone) is a striking white quartz boulder about 3ft high and with a circumference of 6ft 8ins, on your right not far before the track reaches the modern road. In between these two stones is Clap yr Arian (Silver Lump). Two cairns stood here until 1910, when Council workmen destroyed the larger one and carted away its stones for road metal. The circumference of its foundation layer is about 156ft. A Bronze Age axe-hammer, made from spotted blue dolerite from Preseli, came from it.

Dowsing here for the first time in 1988, I recorded the most important ley (this was before the term 'spirit path' became fashionable) as running north-south through Maen Serth. A secondary ley linked Maen Serth with Maengwyngweddw at an angle of about 292 degrees. Returning the next year, I confirmed these dowsed leys. Then, in 1995, a dreamer on Carn Ingli introduced me to a little-known but very useful little book, *The First Stonehenge* by Gaynor Francis. This contained (on page 44) a diagram of what could be termed leys in this area. Only one ran in a line from north to south - it ran south from Maen Serth (SN 943699) through the easternmost of three cairns on Carn Gafallt (SN 943644) to a cairn on Y Gamriw (SN 943614). This was the line I had dowsed!

The importance of this north-south line could also be shown by the map on page 57 of John Michell and Christine Rhone's book (published in 1991). Their line runs southwards to the coast at Llantwit Major, where there was a perpetual choir at St Illtud's famous school around AD 500. I would refine this line so that it reaches the coast slightly further west at St Donats, where a Christian church was built by the daughter of Caractacus in the first century. This interesting line's first point, south of Maen Serth, is Carn Gafallt, which is associated with Cabal, King Arthur's dog, according to Jennifer Westwood's book *Albion*.

As for the line between Maen Serth and Maengwyngweddw, its 292 degrees would link it to sunset in early May (Beltane) and early August (Lugnasadh). It could be extended westwards to the site of a Celtic monastic community near Pont ar Elan.

Route

(Mile 0) With your back to St Winifred's Church, go left along the B4518 for half a mile. Turn right up a signposted bridleway, soon ignoring a waymarked footpath on your right. Take a gate ahead to enter woodland which has been subject to clear-felling. Continue through a second gate into surviving oak woodland.

(Mile 1) Bear right at a fork and keep near a fence on your right. Turn left in a corner, ignoring a gate ahead. Reach an access lane at Middle Ochr-cefn and go down it, soon passing a grassy track on your left. Bear right with the lane and turn left along a track to Treheslog Farm **(Mile 2)**.

Turn right at the farmhouse to pass farm buildings on your left and walk along the foot of the hill on your left and with a view of a lake (Gwynllyn) over the fence on your right. Bear left at a fork near waterfalls (worth diverting to) and climb with a stream (Nant Gwynllyn) on your right **(Mile 3)**.

Meet a path coming from your left and go right to cross the stream and reach a road near a 1:10 road sign. Go left, uphill, a few yards and turn sharply right along a signposted bridleway **(Mile 4)**.

Converge with grassy tracks coming from your right, then left.

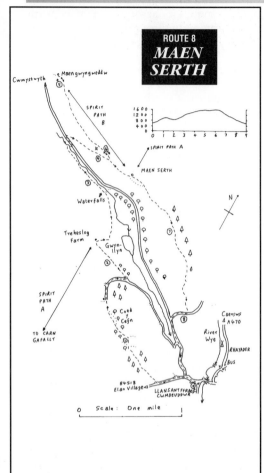

ROUTE 8
MAEN SERTH

Divert sharply left to follow Spirit Path B to the white, quartz stone on your right known as Maengwyngweddw (White-widow Stone) - **(Mile 5)**.

Retrace your steps to the track junction **(Mile 6)** and go ahead, in an easterly direction (towards Rhayader), and soon pass the prominent standing stone known as Maen Serth on your left. Go ahead to descend with the track and pass a forestry plantation on your left **(Mile 7)**.

Turn right down a lane **(Mile 8)** and go left at a junction, then left again with the B4518 to return to Llansantffraed-Cwmdeuddrw, where the church is on your right **(Mile 9)**.

ROUTE 9
DRYGARN FAWR

Distance:	9 miles
Start:	Telephone box at Rhiwnant, grid ref.: SN 901616
OS Maps:	Explorer 200, Landranger 147 (Elan Valley)
Public Transport:	None. There is a postbus to Elan Village from Llandrindod, the nearest railway station (tel. 01597 826642).

Introduction

When going from one reality to another it is often necessary to traverse a desert. If you are blessed, there will be a narrow path in which to tread. So it is when you make a pilgrimage to the sacred heart of Wales.

To the Ancients this was a special zone, as Gaynor Francis conveys in her book *The First Stonehenge*. This author prefaces her book by saying that her original intention was purely to describe her walks in these hills. As is often the case for those who are receptive, the spirit of the land held her and moved her into writing about much more.

Mesolithic hunters in the post-glacial period from about 9000 BC to 4000 BC used the 2103ft summit of Drygarn Fawr as a seasonal clock. There should be three cairns on this peak, according to its name, but only two have survived. Perhaps the third cairn is on Drygarn Fach, a mile away to the south-west.

Drygarn Fawr offers a 360 degree panorama encompassing the hills of Shropshire, the Black Mountains, the Brecon Beacons, the Carmarthen Fannau, Preseli and Pumlumon. Intervening hilltops present themselves as closer marker promontories to exact points on the horizon of astronomical significance. These provided Ancient Man with an accurate calendar. In the case of Carn Gafallt, for example, the hilltop alignment was enhanced by the building of cairns. So developed the guide-lines in the landscape. Stand on Drygarn Fawr and see the sunrise from behind Carn Gafallt (50 degrees) and you'll know it's midsummer. Stand on Carn Gafallt and watch the sunset behind Drygarn Fawr (230 degrees) and you'll know it's the winter solstice.

This walk concentrates on this solstice alignment, which would also seem to have touched the house of prayer believed to have

Approaching Drygarn Fawr from the east

belonged to Cistercian monks from Strata Florida Abbey and now under the waters of Dolymynach Reservoir. Another obvious line, referring to sunrise and sunset at the equinoxes, links Drygarn Fawr with the stone circle passed on this walk at Bwlch y Ddau Ffaen. As Gaynor Francis has shown, however, nearly all the meaningful sun and moon alignments can be made from Drygarn Fawr. This is a rare privilege granted by Nature to a single spot. Drygarn Fawr is the hub of a mighty wheel. A modern play on words just happens to conjure up a picture of a great dragon. Is this a concentration of spirit coiled around Drygarn Fawr, radiating out in all directions?

Route

(Mile 0) Take the no-through road running southwards behind the telephone box and cross the bridge over the Afon Claerwen. At a fork, bear right and go sharply right around a hairpin bend along a lane signposted as a bridleway. After 150 yards fork left through a gate and continue upstream with Rhiwnant on your right. This valley bears right as you climb up Cwm Paradwys **(Mile 1)**.

When the track turns sharply left at a hairpin bend, go straight ahead, keeping the stream (Nant Paradwys) on your right. Follow the well-trodden path which diverges from the stream **(Mile 2)** and leads to a stone circle at Bwlch y Ddau Ffaen.

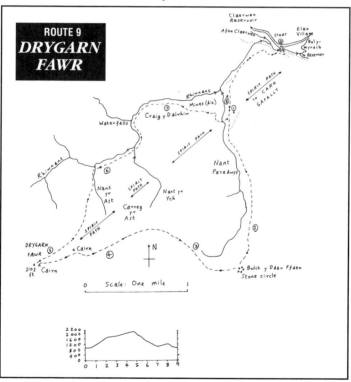

Turn right to walk west, passing a concrete pillar. Skirt the boggy ground on your left **(Mile 3)** and aim for the eastern cairn of Drygarn Fawr **(Mile 4)**. A clear path takes you up to this and on to the western cairn. Beyond this is a trig point.

Turn sharply right to head north-east **(Mile 5)** to the valley of Nant yr Ast. Cross this stream fairly low down, but above the point where it meets the Rhiwnant **(Mile 6)**.

Go right to walk downstream with the Rhiwnant on your left. Continue across Nant yr Ych to reach the ruined buildings of an old lead mine **(Mile 7)**.

Bear right along a track that leads uphill. You soon reach the track you followed on your outward journey **(Mile 8)**. Turn left to retrace your steps to the telephone box **(Mile 9)**.

Distance:	6½ miles
Start:	Space for considerate parking beside forest road near its junction with the minor road north-west of Ditchyeld Bridge, grid ref.: SO 278609
OS Maps:	Explorer 201, Landranger 137 or 148
Public Transport:	Support the new bus from Llandrindod to Evenjobb (SO 263623), tel. 01597 826642. Join this route along the minor road shortly after Mile 1, less than one mile east of Evenjobb.

Introduction

The lines shown on the maps for this walk are marked as leys, not spirit paths. Instead of selecting one such alignment and following it through the countryside, this is a short walk which is crossed by a total of 14 leys. A good test of dowsing would be to take a friend who is unaware of these leys and ask him or her to stop whenever the ley is crossed. The friend who drove me to the start of this walk is a dowser and it was satisfying when she did, indeed, identify these leys as we came upon them. She did not know when to expect them.

Leys and spirit paths are the same thing to me - whatever that is! When I dowse for them I picture a straight shining path, rather like a sunbeam. Words may fail us, but there's no doubting their reality, especially when you open yourself to their presence and, whilst on a walk, suddenly register in your head that you have crossed one. Dowsing with rods can confirm its direction so that a line can be drawn on a map. Then, and only then, consult the map in Chapter III (Leys in Radnor Vale) of Alfred Watkins' seminal book *The Old Straight Track*. Isn't it a wonder to discover that you have dowsed the same line as Watkins drew on his map?

Watkins found his leys by connecting mounds, standing stones and other markers. He devoted a whole chapter to the leys in Radnor Vale because he considered it more convincing to study the ley system in one compact district. He certainly struck a golden vein around this section of Offa's Dyke. Is this because of the surrounding volcanic hills, whose jagged outlines make this such an attractive walk? The sense of vitality here may not be measurable to scientists, but it is readily acknowledged by many people. Is this

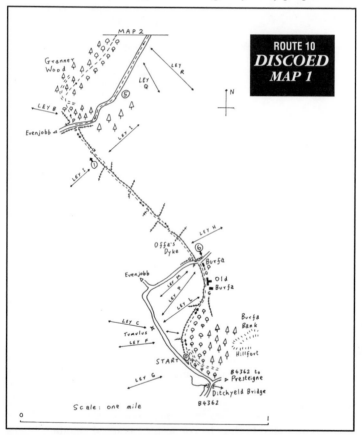

also why marking points for leys are so thick on the ground here? Two straight sections of Offa's Dyke correspond to leys (Watkins' O and Q). *The Old Straight Track* is required reading anyway, but especially so for this route.

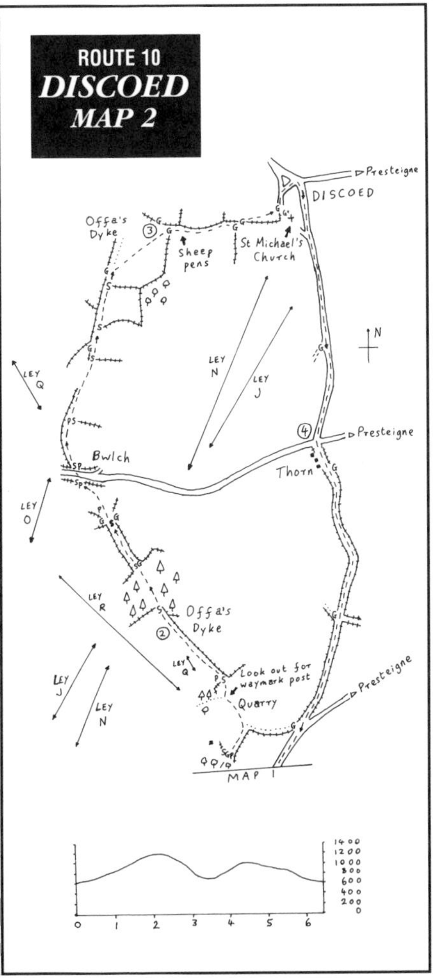

ROUTE 10
DISCOED
MAP 2

Its third chapter is a reminder of how thick leys are on the ground. When following a single ley, of course, it is important to shut out all others by concentrating on it only.

Watkins' ley N goes to St Michael's Church, Discoed. This is a significant dedication. St Michael slays or tames the raw dragon energy of the spirit force in the leys and puts it to good use. Discoed also has an ancient yew tree. It overlooks the River Lug. This river is named after the sun-god, Llew or Lugh the long-handed or silver-handed. Its meadows were grazed from Lughnasad (1st August) in the sign of Leo, the astronomical character of Lancelot, the Lance of Light.

Route
(Mile 0) Continue up the forest road but when it bends right, take a track straight ahead. Follow this to pass the 14th century long house of Old Burfa (a

reference to a grazing place) on your right. Reach a lane, go left and immediately turn right to cross a stile giving access to Offa's Dyke. Walk along the top of its bank, going ahead over a series of stiles waymarked with the acorn emblem of the Offa's Dyke Path national trail. Reach a minor road **(shortly after Mile 1)**. This comes from the bus stop, west at Evenjobb.

Cross the road and follow the signposted Offa's Dyke Path up steps ahead. Continue across a forest road to follow a path which runs along a shelf near the top of Granner Wood. Go round the head of the steep valley on your left and pass a quarry on your right. Look out for a waymark post and bear right near a corrugated iron barn (before the track re-enters the woodland). Climb to a stile, cross it and go ahead with Offa's Dyke towards a forestry plantation **(Mile 2)**.

Follow the waymarked path between the trees and continue to another road. Cross this to continue over five more stiles and, in the fifth field, join a path coming from a gateway on your left (thus leaving Offa's Dyke, the national trail and Watkins' ley O). Bear right to take a gate on your right in the bottom right hand corner of this field **(Mile 3)**.

Continue past sheep pens and with a fence on your left. Take a gate in the corner ahead to the next field. Turn left almost immediately to go through a gate and bear right to the hamlet of Discoed, with its church dedicated to St Michael. Go left, away from the church, bear right at a fork and turn right at a road junction. Climb with a steep lane which passes the church on your right and reaches a T junction **(Mile 4)**.

Go straight ahead along a track which eventually descends to a road. Bear right down the road and **(after Mile 5)** look out for steps and a stile on your left. Turn left to retrace your steps along Offa's Dyke Path **(reaching a lane at Mile 6)** to the start.

Distance:	5¼ miles
Start:	Black Lion Royal Hotel, Lampeter, grid ref.: SN 576482
OS Maps:	Explorer 199, Landranger 146 (Lampeter)
Public transport:	Buses run to Lampeter from Cardiff, Swansea, Bangor & Holyhead (no. 701), Aberaeron & Carmarthen (no. 202), Llandeilo (no. 284), Llandysul (no. 450) and Tregaron (no. 588). Tel. 01545 572504 for details of bus services.

Introduction

Lampeter is a strategic spot in the Teifi valley which can boast the oldest University College in Wales. This has a reputation for religious studies of all faiths, including pagan. Perhaps this reflects the sacred nature of the surrounding landscape, in particular the hills running north-eastwards. Apart from the panoramic views, these are capped by prehistoric hillforts, including Castell Allt-goch.

Visit the grounds of St David's College to see a Norman castle mound which my dowsing revealed to be on a spirit path relating to the moonrise in the northerly minor standstill (60 degrees). Extending this line south-westwards brings it to Peterwell (SN 57104775). Going north-eastwards, this line (Spirit Path A) glances the edge of Lletty-twpa Wood. This wooded hilltop has a very special magical quality and it is characteristic of leys or spirit paths to glance the edge rather than go through the centre of a sacred enclosure.

Climbing to Castell Allt-goch, Spirit Path B runs along the eastern edge of the hillfort and connects the church at Bletws Bledrws in the north (SN 520596) with an old castle mound at SN 591483 to the south.

Spirit Path C was dowsed clipping the western side of Castell Allt-goch and extending northwards to the Derry Ormond Tower

(SN 59005165). Like many such 19th century follies, one wonders whether it was sited on a ley by chance or design.

I extended this walk in a fruitless attempt to find evidence of a lost druidical circle around SN 592502. My dowsing rods could lead me to its presumed site, but not conjure up any surviving stones amongst the stumps of the trees that were planted over it (and more trees have been planted after these were felled). This site does appear

Take this woodland path after Mount Pleasant Farm

on the 1891 OS map (six inches to one mile scale). This is an example of the vandalism suffered by so many sacred sites in the recent past.

The return path goes through Olwen Wood, while Castell Olwen is nearby (SN 580493). The association with Olwen, the Giant's Daughter, is interesting. Read *The Mabinogion* to discover the quest-tale of Culhwch and Olwen. Poor Culhwch was cursed by his stepmother when he refused to marry her daughter. He could only love the archetypal unobtainable woman, Olwen. After a year, with the aid of cousin King Arthur and his knights, Olwen was found, wearing a heavy gold torc. Her father Ysbaddaden, Chief Giant, feared that her marriage would mean his death, so he set the suitor impossibletasks, ratherlike the Labours of Hercules, including fetching the birds of Rhiannon. Culhwch eventually married Olwen, thus enabling the transfer of power from her father

The wishing well, Carn Cŵn (Route 12)

Stone gate posts below Modron (Route 12)

A spirit path leads from Carreg Coetan to Carn Ingli (Route 12)

The Sleeping Giant at Carn Ffoi (Route 12)

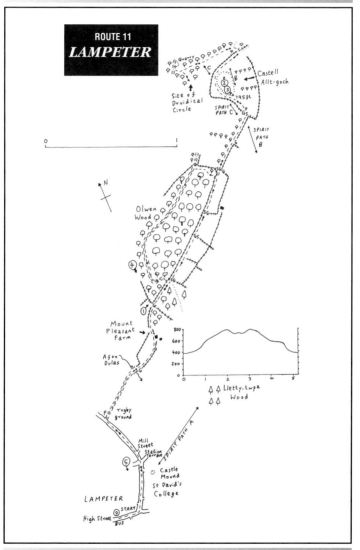

ROUTE 11
LAMPETER

Q.Quarry

Castell
Allt-goch

795ft

C

B

Site of
Druidical
Circle

SPIRIT
PATH C

GS

SPIRIT
PATH
B

N

0 _____ I

Olwen
Wood

GS

GS

④

GS-G

G

①

Mount
Pleasant
Farm

800
600
400
200
0   1   2   3   4   5

△ △ Lletty-twpa
△ △   Wood

Afon
Dulas

P.H. rugby
      ground

Mill
Street
Station Terrace

SPIRIT PATH A

⑤

Castle
Mound
St David's
College

LAMPETER

High Street

⓪ START
BUS

to the young lover. The gift of sovereignty, with implications of potency and prosperity, was Olwen's. Olwen's name means 'White Track', signifying the white clovers that sprang up where she walked.

Route

(Mile 0) Face the Black Lion Royal Hotel and go left along the High Street, then turn left along College Street and pass St David's College (with the castle mound in its grounds) on your right. Continue past Station Terrace and Mill Street on your right, then the rugby ground, before turning right along a signposted bridleway which serves as the access track to Mount Pleasant Farm. Bear left with the waymarked path when you climb up to the farm buildings. Follow this path along the edge of woodland which extends to your right **(Mile 1)**.

Go ahead through a gate to follow the path through the middle of woodland. Pass a stile (over which you will come on your way back) on your left and cross a stile beside a gate to emerge in the corner of a field. Continue with woodland behind a fence on your left and pass four fields on your right. When the woodland on your left ends, go straight ahead over a stile beside a gate to walk with a fence on your right. This leads to another stile which you cross and bear left to pass the hillfort of Castell Allt-goch on your right **(Mile 2)**.

Bear right to walk with a fence on your left to a stile in it. Turn left to follow a path which soon forks left down into woodland. See if you can find, or at least dowse the location of, the lost druidical circle (I shall want to know if you do find it!), then retrace your steps to the hillfort of Castell Allt-goch **(Mile 3)**.

Go back towards Lampeter along the signposted path, crossing the stile beside the gate near the signpost and descending with the fence now on your left. Cross the stile in the next corner and look for another stile within a few yards in the fence on your right. Turn right to cross this and follow a woodland path which leads downhill with the perimeter fence of this wood (Olwen Wood) on your right. Join a firm forest track which comes through a gate on your right. Turn left along it through Olwen Wood and follow it as it bears left to come to a halt near the stile noticed on your outward journey **(Mile 4)**. Bear right to cross this stile and turn right to walk downhill the way you came back into Lampeter.

ROUTE 12
CARN INGLI

Distance:	8½ miles
Start:	Tourist Information Centre, Long Street, Newport (Pembs), grid ref.: SN 057392
OS Maps:	Outdoor Leisure 35 (North Pembrokeshire), Landranger 145 (Cardigan)
Public Transport:	Bus no. 412 (Cardigan - Fishguard - Haverfordwest, tel. 01239 613756 for details)

Introduction

The author of this guidebook was privileged to spend 810 nights dreaming at the 1138ft summit of Carn Ingli from 1993 to 1999. Many of those nights were shared with other dreamers coming from all over the world and hundreds of dreams were tape-recorded. Some of this research is intended for future publication elsewhere. Suffice it to say that the author feels very close to this holy hill and that this is a very special sacred peak. Cast your shoes away and come as an ancient pilgrim, for this is holy ground. Only come if you really do acknowledge and respect the living spirit of this place. Prepare for hardships, jagged rocks, strong winds, lashing rain, impenetrable mists, thunder and lightning, snow and ice and all manner of tests and endurances. Fast and pray. If in despair, seek comfort. Open yourself to the place and you will find yourself in paradise.

The peak's name reflects the fact that St Brynach communed with the angels here in the sixth century. This agile, nimble, bare-footed, smiling, kindly, glowing-all-over contemporary of St David and son-in-law of King Brychan has been seen here in dreams. So have the angels.

A little can be revealed on this walk, which takes in two of the many leys radiating from or converging on Carn Ingli. Look out for several examples of landscape figures. After strangers to the area (who had even ascended the hill in mist, so they had no idea of the shape of the land) had vivid dreams of giants and indicated to me that these mighty beings were in the landscape, I was amazed to discover these Gulliver-like characters formed by the rocks in the expected places. A lady born on the slope of Carn Ingli who also contributed dreams was able to tell me more, her family long being familiar with the giants.

The first encountered on this walk is the Sleeping Giant of Carn Ffoi. This male figure (perhaps Myrddin or Merlin placed in the rocks by Vivien the enchantress) was seen by one dreamer breaking free of the rocks and standing up in a daze, thanks to an earthquake. Is the spirit of the land free at last?

The Sleeping Giant's arms are formed by a stone wall, which suggests sacred landscaping to me but defensive ramparts to archaeologists. It would be a weak spot to defend, being overlooked by higher ground. Dating from the first millennium BC, Carn Ffoi is at grid reference SN 049379. Its name is interesting as Ffoi means 'fleeing'. There happens to be a Pembrokeshire tale about three giants, the last of their race. Two were female and one was male. Instead of happily practising polygamy, the two females fought for the right to be the male's wife and killed each other. The forlorn male fled to the hillside and died of a broken heart. Ffoi may also suggest a fool and a King (roi).

The local dreamer mentioned above was able to show me a figure of a female giant with her legs wide apart, straining in the act of giving birth (the baby's head is apparent). This is best seen in good sunlight from the road above the stone gate posts. This pregnant goddess is at the foot of the Sleeping Giant. Another dreamer was amazed to recognise the stone gate posts at the foot of this giant the morning after she, a stranger to the area, had described them vividly in a dream at the summer solstice of 1994. Later I was to realise a connection between the emerging baby's head and the summer solstice sunset line coming from the ancient monument known as Cerrig y Gof (SN 037389) one mile to the west-north-west. The angle of this line is 310 degrees. Could it be that the goddess giving birth is Modron, the mother-goddess who gave birth to the archetypal divine son Mabon, who was stolen from her when three days old and disappeared for many years (a fate also suffered by Rhiannon)? Does Modron's temporary loss of her son symbolise the cycle of birth, death and rebirth or the seasons of the year? The setting sun at the summer solstice does shine on the head of the baby Mabon.

Not thinking of the summer solstice sunset line when at Cerrig y Gof, I just asked my dowsing rods to show me the primary ley from these burial chambers. It led from Pen Dinas and Cwm yr Eglwys in the west-north-west through the middle of the group of five burial chambers whose name refers to a blacksmith along a line at an angle of 304 degrees. This ley passes Carn Ffoi and one mile east-south-east from the Sleeping Giant comes to the third eye of the Sleeping Goddess of Carn Ingli.

The Sleeping Goddess of Carn Ingli is much bigger than the Sleeping Giant of Carn Ffoi. Both figures have their heads to the south and their feet to the north. The Sleeping Goddess of Carn Ingli appears to be three or four months pregnant. Once again, her arms are formed by a stone wall, as are her legs (or, rather, this should be arm and leg in the singular because her profile can be seen from one side only - the rocks only provide her with one breast, for instance, conforming to this single-sided profile). The archaeologists think these are first millennium BC defensive ramparts, but concede that they may even be Neolithic (the dreams indicate a very early exotic presence). A nearby Iron Age village was destroyed (with much fire) in an attack, probably by Irish invaders. The extraordinary number of entrances suggests a sacred rather than a military purpose to Carn Ingli

Dreams reveal sacred ceremonies, including a severed head atop a pole, in a circle of grass set in the rocky summit of Carn Ingli. This is where St Brynach communed with the angels (and a lush patch of grass marks where an angel stood). It is the navel of the goddess and one dreamer (who did not know that) described seeing a rope through clouds rather like an umbilical cord (instead of a ladder for angels to ascend and descend by). It is surrounded by rocks which spin a magnetic compass, including one very special rock which causes a compass needle to spin virtually the full 360 degrees. I associate this powerful rock with the appearance of the goddess Rhiannon and this lap of the goddess is the most nurturing of spots. If we all have compasses in our heads, this is the place to be disorientated and whirled into other dimensions. It is a gateway to

Annwn, the Celtic Otherworld, especially at certain times. If the navel's umbilical cord leads to heaven in the sky, the exquisitely-shaped rocks below the navel form the vagina and, to certain patriarchal eyes, the entrance to hell.

One night, in a dream, this Sleeping Goddess rose up, dressed in white, to walk up the hillside to me, scattering seeds. When she reached me, she held her cupped hands of seeds and said they were for me.

Descending to the eastern foot of Carn Ingli, turn and look at the profile of a huge, reclining angel. The head is in the south, with the angel's wings folded beneath it as a pillow. Like the other giant figures, it has clasped hands.

With such a feast in store, whet your appetite by visiting the burial chamber of Carreg Coetan near the start of this walk. A ley can be dowsed going from it to glance the eastern side of the goddess' navel at the summit of Carn Ingli. This ley enters Carningli Common through its chief gateway at SN 062383 and runs south of Carn Ingli past a standing stone at SN 064351 on its way to the summit of Cerrig Lladron, where there is a cairn at SN 066321.

After following the Pembrokeshire Coast Path, reach Cerrig y Gof. This cluster of five burial chambers dates from at least 3000 BC. I first dowsed our second ley which runs through Cerrig y Gof to the third eye of the Sleeping Goddess of Carn Ingli on the eve of the summer solstice of 1995. That night there were five of us dreaming in the navel of the goddess. I stayed awake to tape-record the others and C was the first to signal a dream at 2am. 'She is there', he said. Unknown to him, the moon rose at that moment behind the sleeping C's shoulder. C then went on to dream of a hammer shattering a rock into five small pieces. Much later N had a dream of the goddess' hand pushing five small pieces of rock into the ground where they changed into seedlings. N, of course, had been sound asleep and isolated when C had been whispering his earlier dream into my tape-recorder. Snatching the chance for some sleep myself around 5am, I came in a dream to a detached view of the five of us (including my own body), forming a circle as we slept. A single word was heard - 'pray'. Were the five of us on Carn Ingli that midsummer night the five pieces of rock, turning into seedlings as the goddess' fingers pushed us into the soil? Why are there five burial chambers at Cerrig y Gof (Rocks of the Smith)? Were our souls being hammered into shape?

The wishing well in the rocks of Carn Cŵn may mark another entrance to Annwn, being the home of the Cŵn Annwn (the Hounds of the Otherworld).

Route

(Mile 0) Face the Tourist Information Centre in Long Street and go right to the crossroads in the centre of Newport. Turn left along East Street, pass the Golden Lion pub on your left and turn left down Pen-y-Bont.

NB. THE START IS ON MAP 2 - PAGE 88

Divert left, as signposted, to Carreg Coetan burial chamber.

Resume your previous direction to reach the bridge over the Afon Nyfer. Without crossing it, turn left along the signposted Pembrokeshire Coast Path, with the estuary on your right **(Mile 1)**. Keep with the Coast Path past the harbour and the lifeboat station, climb the clifftop path and walk with the sea on your right **(Mile 2)**.

Turn left over a stile to take a signposted path inland. Reach the A487 and divert right along it to cross a bridge, pass a house on your right and come to a gate on your right. This gives access to Cerrig y Gof **(Mile 3)**.

With your back to Cerrig y Gof, go left along the A487 until you can turn right up the access track for Hendre. Pass this farmhouse on your right to follow the waymarked path to a stile straddling a wall ahead. Cross the stile and go ahead to climb with a wall on your right and emerge on Ffordd Bedd Morris.

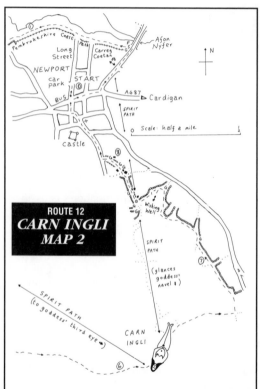

Go right up the road, soon forking left. Note a house called Treffynnon on your right **(Mile 4)** and the stone gate posts on your left immediately after it. You will return to these gate posts. First, continue up the road to where it bends right across a bridge.

Turn around to enjoy views of the Sleeping Giant of Carn Ffoi on your right as you descend. Turn right when you reach the stone gate posts and go through them to walk below the feet of the Sleeping Giant (where the goddess Modron may be seen giving birth to Mabon). Walk near a wall on your left. Shortly after coming to the end of a plantation of conifer trees behind the wall on your left, take the well-trodden path which turns right uphill. Pass the back of the Sleeping Giant's head on your right **(Mile 5)**. Walk with a wall on your left. Keep climbing to a gap in a wall ahead, where a stone has 'Carreg Sam' painted on it.

Take the gap to climb above this wall. Reach the jagged rocks of Carnedd Fychan and bear left across the plateau of Carningli Common towards the profile of the Sleeping Goddess of Carn Ingli **(Mile 6)**. Approach this figure at the southern end, near her head. Climb down her body, passing her navel.

When level with the Sleeping Goddess' knee, turn right to descend towards a road. Don't go quite to it. Turn left at a waymarked path junction just above the road. Continue with a wall on your right **(Mile 7)**, ignoring downhill paths until the wall turns right and the rocks of Carn Cwn appear on your left. Descend to the gate in the bottom right corner but don't take it. Turn left to walk along the foot of Carningli Common and divert left with a path through the bracken towards the wishing well hidden by the rocks of Carn Cwn.

Return to the foot of Carningli Common and go left to walk with the wall on your right. Turn right through a gate to walk down a track. Fork right at a junction and reach a road **(Mile 8)**.

Go right downhill into Newport. Pass below the castle on your left and St Mary's Church on your right. Bear left with West Street to a crossroads and turn right down Market Street back to the centre of Newport. The bus stops are in Bridge Street on your left, while the Tourist Information Centre and the car park are straight ahead down Long Street.

Distance:	16 miles (which can be divided into a southern circuit of 4½ miles and a northern circuit of 11½ miles at Felindre Farchog)
Start:	Salutation Inn, Felindre Farchog, grid ref.: SN100390
OS Maps:	Outdoor Leisure 35 (North Pembrokeshire), Landranger 145 (Cardigan)
Public Transport:	Bus no. 412 runs to Felindre Farchog from Cardigan, Newport, Fishguard and Haverfordwest (tel. 01239 613756)

Introduction

It was around Pentre Ifan burial chamber that W.Y. Evans Wentz recorded sightings of fairies in *The Fairy Faith in Celtic Countries*. Guarded by the giant in the volcanic rocks of Carnedd Meibion-Owen and at the eastern edge of the magical woodland where ghosts of chanting Druids and visions of Pan or Cernunnos have been seen, Pentre Ifan is one of the most important megalithic monuments in Wales. Dating from 4000 BC, its tapering, pointed, uprights support a heavy capstone. This walk follows a spirit path dowsed as running just a degree or two off the north-south line. Another spirit path leads to the summit of Carn Ingli, seen in the west through the frame of the uprights and capstone.

The northern end of this spirit path is the Witches Cauldron (Pwll y Wrach). This scenic highlight of the Pembrokeshire Coast Path is an enlarged and collapsed blowhole. A classic feature of marine erosion, its access arch was the original cave. Is this where King Arthur landed with a cauldron full of the treasures of Ireland, according to the story of Culhwch and Olwen? *The Mabinogion* tale states that this was at Mesur-y-Peir (measure of the Cauldron) in Dyfed. Just inland of the Witches Cauldron is an Iron Age hillfort (Castell-treruffydd).

About one mile inland, going south along the spirit path, is Llech y Dribedd burial chamber. Its name refers to its 'tripod' nature.

Another spirit path can be dowsed here, going to the summit of Carn Ingli. Line this burial chamber up with the sacred peak in the (south-western) background and you can see how the shape of the capstone when seen from that angle resembles the shape of Carn Ingli behind it. There is a legend that St Samson (the nephew of King Arthur) threw the stones of Llech y Dribedd to this spot from Carn Ingli.

The second edition (1907) OS six inches to one mile maps of this area indicate earthworks along this spirit path at about SN 100411 and SN 101416. Wandering not far off the line are a cup-marked rock at SN 103403 and the abandoned church dedicated to St Andrew at SN 102406. The dowser Hamish Miller and Paul Broadhurst have written in *The Sun and the Serpent* about Michael and Mary (male and female) currents coiling around the great spirit path or ley of the Dragon Line, which runs from Cornwall to Norfolk by way of Glastonbury Tor and Avebury. Could such currents coiling around this line pass through these sites which are so near the straight line of the spirit path? My dowsing at the cup-marked rock showed that it was on a spirit path running westwards to Dinas Head.

Well off the spirit path, but beside the road as you descend to Nevern, near the end of this walk, are the ruins of Castell Nanhyfer. A motte and bailey were built here by Robert Fitz Martin, Norman Lord of Cemais, in the 12th century. It was held temporarily by the Welsh prince Rhys ap Gruffudd and his sons between 1191 and 1204.

Descending to where the road bends left before Nevern, divert right for 35 yards along the footpath (and old pilgrims' path on the route between Holywell and St David's). Look on your right to see a wayside cross cut in the rock with a kneeling ledge and a hand-grip. Shaded by trees, this spot has retained a very special sanctity. It has also, I believe, featured in dreams experienced on Carn Ingli. In October 1994, a dreamer described an old woman (56 years old) giving birth to a female 'angel-child' (glowing all over) in a cave. The dreamer, who was not a local, pointed out the direction of this cave from the summit of Carn Ingli. This happened to be towards Nevern. Meeting local author and expert on the Celts John Sharkey the next day, I enquired about caves in this area. He told me that a cave had, indeed, been discovered that summer beneath Nevern's Pilgrims' Cross. It had soon been re-sealed, but the outline of a cave entrance can be traced below this cross. Some say this cave once contained, or still does contain, a fragment of the true cross. Was this the cave of the dream on Carn Ingli? John Sharkey also pointed out that the hag of our dream could relate to the white pregnant sow that St Brynach was 'directed by angels' (saw in a dream?) to follow and build his church on the site where she gave birth (see John Sharkey's *Pilgrim Ways*). The saint did build his church just around the corner from the wayside cross and cave in Nevern. Different dreamers, unaware of each other and the previous dreams, as well as being strangers to the area, added to the story of this birth in a cave in the direction of Nevern at intervals leading up to Christmas 1994. Christmas brings an obvious link with a holy birth in a cave. Interestingly, I then learned of a legend that every Christmas Eve the Star of Bethlehem is said to rise over Carn Ingli and shine on Nevern's Pilgrims' Cross.

St Brynach's Church, Nevern, is a very special church. Its churchyard gate faces Carn Ingli and a spirit path extends from that angelic mountain's summit through an old horse-mounting block and the churchyard wall to glance the second yew tree on your right as you walk towards the church. This tree is the famous Bleeding Yew Tree. Look at its bleeding stump on the side hidden from the path. It is best in the spring, when other yews nearby can also be observed to bleed, but bleeds throughout the year. It is said that to dip your fingers in its blood, then lick it, touch your eyes and anoint your 'third eye' will make you psychic. One legend is that a monk was hung from this tree for rape. He protested his innocence and predicted that the tree would bleed evermore as proof.

The spirit path from Carn Ingli leads to the High Cross. Dating from around 1000, this impressive structure stands 10 feet high and has intricate Celtic knotwork carvings. Too late to be associated with St Brynach, there is a story that the exhausted St David left it here for his friend on his way back from the synod at Llanddewi Brefi. The wheelhead is softer sandstone whose nearest source is St David's Head, so this may explain that link. St Brynach came to this area around 540 and spent three years communing with the angels on Carn Ingli. During that time, after the Battle of Camlan, Derfel Gadarn joined him for a while. The Pendragon then was Maelgwn

Gwynedd who, after visiting Brynach's monastery, exempted the saint for ever from all royal tribute. Brynach was an Irishman who married Corth, or Cymorth, a daughter of Brychan of Brycheiniog. He was this ruler's chaplain at Llanfrynach before leaving his wife and four children and coming to Carn Ingli. He must have known the Goddess of Carn Ingli and there is a legend of a woman giving him wolf's-bane as a love potion. Brynach eventually moved on to North Devon where his bones lie under the altar of the church he founded at Braunton. St Brynach's Day is 7th April and there is a legend that the service would not start on that day until a cuckoo had sung on the High Cross. This would make sense if the date were amended to 18th April, to allow for the change in the calendar. One year the legendary cuckoo was delayed because of bad weather. Eventually the faithful bird (sacred to Rhiannon) arrived, exhausted. It sang the obligatory note so that the service could begin, then expired.

Enter the church and go to the window sills on the right-hand side of the nave. One bears a memorial stone carved in Latin and Ogham to Maelgwn (Maglocunus), son of Clutorius. Dated to the sixth century AD, this could commemorate a local ruler or it might even be the gravestone of the Pendragon who granted Brynach exemption from tribute - the great Maelgwn Gwynedd (son of Cadwallon - how would that be rendered in Latin?). The next window sill bears a stone with what is known as a carved cross. Look at it carefully and you may make out the form of the goddess.

Nevern has a long history and appears to have been the most important settlement in this area until the Fitz Martins built their castle at Newport when Castell Nanhyfer (Nevern Castle) was lost to the Welsh in 1191. Notice the memorial stone outside the church, near the porch. This dates from the fifth century AD and is for Vitalianus 'Emereto' (discharged with honour?). It is possible that Vitalianus was Vortigern's son, Vortimer, who was also known as Vitalianus. His father was the traitor Vortigern who invited the Saxons into Kent in return for the hand of Rowena, the daughter of Hengist. In the battles that followed as a result, Vortimer fought bravely against the Saxons but was poisoned by his step-mother Rowena.

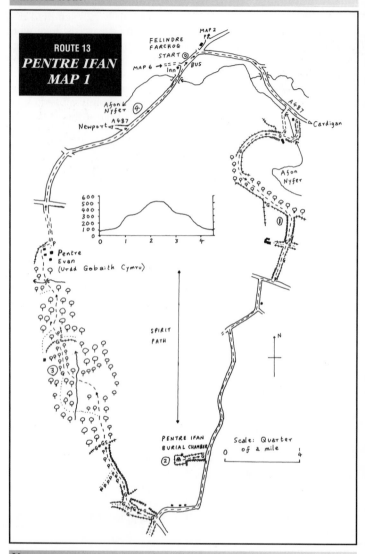

ROUTE 13
*PENTRE IFAN
MAP 1*

FELINDRE
FARCHOG
MAP 6 → START ⓪
Inn BUS

MAP 2
PP

A487 Cardigan

Afon
Nyfer ④

Newport ← A487

Afon
Nyfer

①

16

Pentre
Evan
(Urdd Gobaith Cymru)

③

SPIRIT
PATH

N

PENTRE IFAN
BURIAL CHAMBER
②

Scale: Quarter
of a mile
0   1
       4

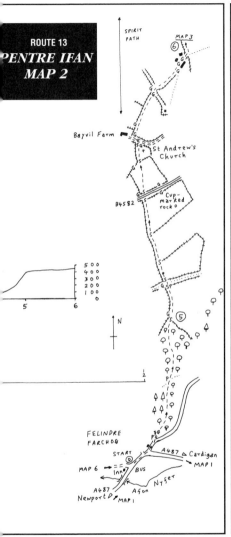

ROUTE 13
PENTRE IFAN
MAP 2

SPIRIT
PATH

MAP 3

⑥

Bayvil Farm

St Andrew's
Church

B4582

Cup-
marked
rock ○

500
400
300
200
100
0

5   6

↑ N

1
2

⑤

FELINDRE
FARCHOG

START
⑨

MAP 6 →   Inn   Bus

A487
Newport P   Afon
         MAP 1   Nyfer

A487 △ Cardigan
         MAP 1

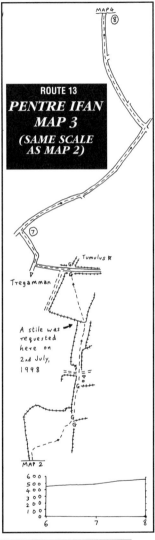

MAP 4

⑧

ROUTE 13
PENTRE IFAN
MAP 3
(SAME SCALE
AS MAP 2)

⑦

Tumulus ⊼

Tregamman

A stile was
requested
here on
2nd July,
1998

MAP 2

600
500
400
300
200
100
0

6   7   8

Route

(Mile 0) With your back to the Salutation Inn, Felindre Farchog, go left along the main road (there will soon be a verge on the right-hand side of the road). Ignore minor roads forking left, pass a farm access lane on your right and a few yards after it turn right through a gate to follow the public bridleway which crosses the Afon Nyfer by a footbridge and emerges at Wenallt. Join the lane coming from your right and turn left to follow what soon becomes a muddy, hedged track. Bear left to follow the path along the top of woodland sloping down on your left, then bear right with a walled track which leads to a minor road **(Mile 1)**.

Turn right and take the next turning on your left. Bear right at a fork and follow the road as it bends left at the next one (where a farm track forks right). Go ahead along the road until a lay-by and a sign on your right indicating the access path for Pentre Ifan burial chamber **(Mile 2)**.

After visiting Pentre Ifan, go right to resume your former direction up the road. Reach a crossing of the road, which bends left, and tracks. Turn right across a cattle grid and follow the track past one gate in the fence on your right. Bear right through the second gate to take the signposted path. Follow this into the woodland and keep to the waymarked route (a permissive one, but the public bridleway is less popular with the local naturalists). Bear right where this re-joins the right of way **(Mile 3)**.

Follow the tree-lined path to a gate giving access to more woodland. Go through this and, ignoring a stile on your right, bear left to join a track and bear right along it to pass the old court of Pentre Evan. This is now a holiday centre for the Urdd Gobaith Cymru (Welsh Youth League). Follow its access lane to a road and cross this to take the road ahead. Descend and bear right with this to join the A487 **(Mile 4)**. Bear right and cross the bridge over the river to return to the Salutation Inn, Felindre Farchog.

Pass the Salutation Inn on your left and fork left with the road to Moylgrove. Soon bear left along a track which enters woodland. Go ahead as signposted, climbing to emerge over a stile in the corner of a field **(Mile 5)**.

Go ahead along the left-hand side of the field, cross a lane and continue along the left-hand sides of three more fields (notice the

Capel-y-ffin Church reminded the Reverend Francis Kilvert of an owl (Route 15)

Looking along the ley north-westwards from Cerig y Gof towards Dinas Head (Route 12)

Walking towards Llandrillo from Bwlch Maen Gwynedd (Route 3)

cup-marked rock away to your right in the third field). Cross the B4582 and bear slightly right when going through the field ahead to reach a stile giving access to an enclosed area which contains the redundant St Andrew's Church. Pass this on your right. Go left along the access track towards Bayvil Farm and turn right to walk along the left-hand side of a field. Ignoring what appears to be a hedged track going left and right, go ahead to bear right along the right-hand edge of a field to a farmyard. Pass through this and turn left to walk along the left-hand edge of the next field **(Mile 6)**.

Bear right to the left-hand of two gates near the far right corner. Take this gate and turn left. Continue across a lane and go ahead up a long, narrow, field. Cross the fence ahead and bear left to reach a road. Go left, turn right when the access lane for Tregamman goes left, then turn right at the next road junction, signposted for Moylgrove **(Mile 7)**.

Turn left at the next crossroads and soon pass access lanes for Llainwen and Fagwreinion Fawr on your right **(Mile 8)**. Continue past Penlanfach on your left, go left at the next road junction and immediately turn right to resume walking northwards towards the sea **(Mile 9)**. Reach the coast and turn left with the signposted Pembrokeshire Coast Path. Walk with the sea on your right **(Mile 10)** and cross the natural arch forming the entrance to Pwll y Wrach (Witches Cauldron), on your left.

Follow the waymarked Coast Path over a footbridge and bear right uphill to a path junction. Ignoring the stile ahead (taken by the Coast Path), turn left to cross a stile just before it and walk inland, passing the site of Castell-treruffydd and keeping above a wooded valley on your left. Reach Treriffith, where you go right to pass the farm buildings, then turn left along the access track to a road **(Mile 11)**.

Go right along the road until the first lane (giving access to Penlan) on your left. Turn left up this and leave the lane to bear left for Penlan while you go straight ahead with the fenced track. Bear left at a fork to visit Llech y Drybedd burial chamber, approached by crossing a stile on your right. Retrace your steps to the fork and turn left along the fenced track to resume your previous direction. Bear left at the next fork **(Mile 12)**.

Continue past the buildings of Treicert on your left to take its

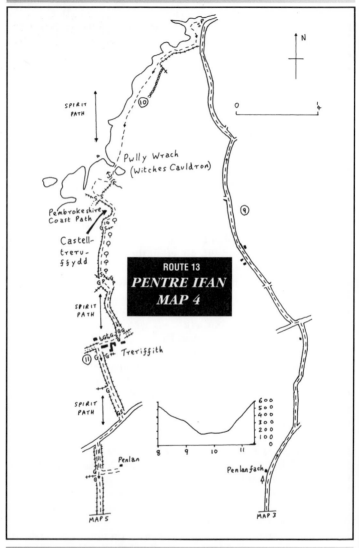

SPIRIT
PATH

Pwlly Wrach
(Witches Cauldron)

Pembrokeshire
Coast Path

Castell-
treru-
ffydd

ROUTE 13
PENTRE IFAN
MAP 4

SPIRIT
PATH

Treriffith

SPIRIT
PATH

Penlan

Penlanfach

MAP 5

MAP 3

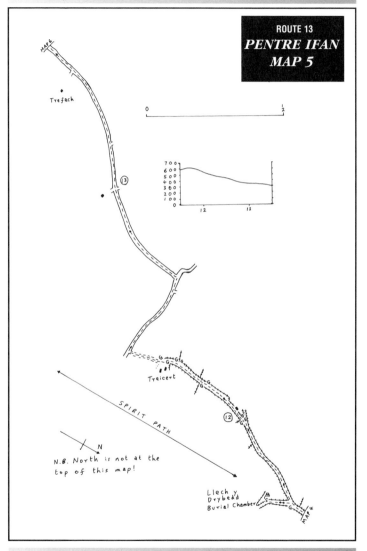

ROUTE 13
PENTRE IFAN
MAP 5

MAP 6

Trefach

0   1
                     2

13

700
600
500
400
300
200
100
0
        12   13

L

G
G
G
Treicert
G
G

SPIRIT PATH

12
G
G

N

N.B. North is not at the
top of this map!

Llech y
Drybedd
Burial Chamber
m
S
G
MAP 4

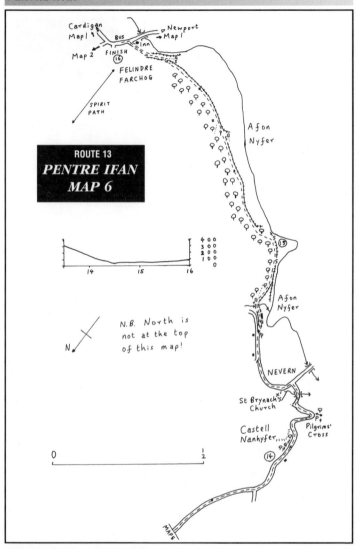

Cardigan
Map 1

Newport
Map 1

BUS

Inn

Map 2

FINISH
(16)

FELINDRE
FARCHOG

SPIRIT
PATH

ROUTE 13
PENTRE IFAN
MAP 6

Afon
Nyfer

400
300
200
100

14   15   16

(15)

15

Afon
Nyfer

N.B. North is
not at the top
of this map!

N

NEVERN

St Brynach's
Church

Castell
Nanhyfer

Pilgrims'
Cross

(14)

0   1
                     2

MAP 5

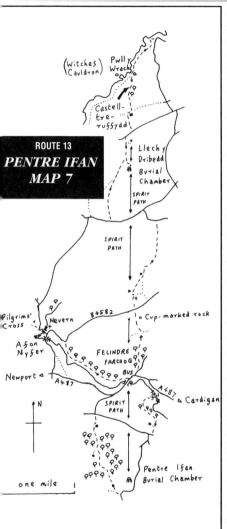

ROUTE 13
**PENTRE IFAN
MAP 7**

access lane ahead to a road. Turn right along this and take the first turning on your left, signposted as the road for Nevern **(Mile 13)**. Pass the site of Castell Nanhyfer on your left as you descend with the road towards Nevern **(Mile 14)**. Divert along the signposted path on your right when the road bends left down to Nevern. Follow this path for 35 yards to find the wayside Pilgrims' Cross carved in the rock on your right. Retrace your steps to the bend in the road and go downhill to Nevern. Cross a bridge, go left to visit the church and continue along the road which passes the church on your left. Look for a signposted bridleway which forks right. Take this to cross a footbridge and follow the ancient pilgrims' route along the foot of a wooded slope on your left, keeping the meadows of the Afon Nyfer on your right **(Mile 15)**. Follow this path back to Felindre Farchog, where the Salutation Inn appears on your right **(Mile 16)**.

Distance:	7 miles
Start:	Statue of the Duke of Wellington, Brecon, grid ref.: SO 045285
OS Maps:	Outdoor Leisure 12 (Brecon Beacons West & Central), Landranger 160 (Brecon Beacons)
Public Transport:	Buses run to Brecon from Hereford (39 & 40), Abergavenny (20 & 29), Merthyr Tydfil and Cardiff (43), Swansea (63, 120 & 760) and Llandrindod (47) - all places with railway stations. Tel. 01597 826642 for details (or 01874 623156 for details of buses on summer Sundays and Bank Holiday Mondays).

Introduction

Appendix D of *The Old Straight Track* by Alfred Watkins is devoted to a study of the leys to the west of Brecon. These leys can be dowsed as spirit paths and four of them are visited on this walk. Ley A on my maps runs from Twyn y Gaer (SN 970306) along the southern side of the Roman fort at Y Gaer, glances the southern edge of the hillfort in Coed Fenni-fach and passes over the site of the old castle in Brecon on its way to Cathedine church.

Ley B goes along the northern edge of the roman fort at Y Gaer, clips the northern side of the hillfort in Coed Fenni-fach and passes just to the north of Brecon cathedral (where there is a holy well) on its way to Llangorse church. Ley C runs north-eastwards from a motte or castle mound at SN 956261, then clips the southern sides of Twyn y Gaer (SN 990280), the hillfort in Coed Fenni-fach and the hillfort of Pen y Crug. Ley D follows a similar course but glances the northern edges of the earthworks passed by Ley C. Maen-du holy well, near the end of the walk, was where love-lorn maids offered pins in the hope of future romance.

Route

(Mile 0) Go along Brecon's High Street, passing the statue of the Duke of Wellington and St Mary's Church on your left. Continue down Ship Street, approach the bridge over the River Usk but turn right just before it. Cross the Afon Honddu, go left and turn right to follow the riverside promenade upstream with the Usk on your left. Reach a toposcope overlooking a weir near a car park. Pen-y-Fan (2907ft) can be viewed to the south.

    Go left along a road, but very soon fork right. A signposted

Follow this bridleway to Y Gaer, west of Brecon

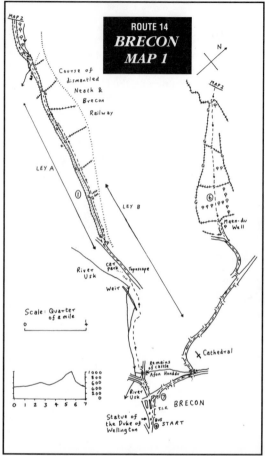

ROUTE 14
BRECON
MAP 1

N

MAP 2

Course of
dismantled
Neath &
Brecon
Railway

LEY A

LEY B

MAP 2

Maen-du
Well

River
Usk

Car
Park   Toposcope

Weir

Scale: Quarter
of a mile

0   ¼

Cathedral

1000
800
600
400
200
0

0 1 2 3 4 5 6 7

Remains
of castle
Afon Honddu

River
Usk   BRECON

T.I.C.

Statue of
the Duke of   BUS
Wellington   START

bridleway runs in the shade between hedges. Turn right over a stile just before its first gate, then turn left to walk with a fieldpath running parallel to the bridleway **(Mile 1)**. The course of the dismantled Neath & Brecon Railway is away to your right. In the fourth field, bear left to continue with the bridleway **(Mile 2)** and take it to Y Gaer, where visitors to the Roman fort are asked not to bring dogs **(Mile 3)**.

Turn right across Y Gaer's access lane and follow a signposted fieldpath down to the Afon Ysgir.

Walk upstream with this river on your left to a bridge, which you don't cross. Turn right along a road and go ahead at the crossroads in Cradoc **(Mile 4)**. Pass a golf club on your left, climb to a lay-by on your left and look out for a track on your right. Turn right up this track **(Mile 5)**, climbing to open moorland. Enjoy fine views from Pen y Crug hilllfort and continue down to a stile waymarked with a yellow arrow near a corner in a fence shaded by trees. Cross the stile to follow the yellow arrows downhill to the edge of Brecon, where you find an enchanting holy well (Maen-du) on your left **(Mile 6)**. Bear left along the perimeter road of a housing estate. This leads to the B4520 on your left. Turn right to walk along the pavement of this road downhill into Brecon (diverting to visit the cathedral on your left). Cross the Afon Honddu, go right and bear left back up the High Street **(Mile 7)**.

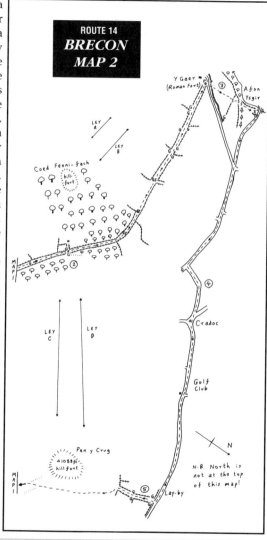

ROUTE 14
*BRECON
MAP 2*

Y Gaer
(Roman Fort)

Afon Ysgir

LEY A

LEY B

Coed Fenni-Fach
hill fort

MAP 1

MAP 2

LEY C

LEY D

Cradoc

Golf Club

N

N.B. North is not at the top of this map!

Pen y Crug
△1088ft
hill fort

MAP 1

Lay-by

Distance:	7¼ miles
Start:	Gospel Pass car park, grid ref.: SO 236351
OS Maps:	Outdoor Leisure 13 (Brecon Beacons East), Landranger 161 (Abergavenny)
Public Transport:	None. Nearest bus stop in Hay-on-Wye (nos 39 & 40, Hereford - Brecon, tel. 01633 266336 or 01597 826642) six miles to the north of Gospel Pass.

Introduction

Before walking this route and dowsing its spirit path, I dreamt with G, a veteran of dreaming on Carn Ingli, at Bleanau stone circle (SO 239373). This is next to a car park beside the road leading south from Hay-on-Wye to Gospel Pass. Dating from the late third millennium BC, this is probably the oldest evidence for the recognition of the sacred nature of this area.

During that night G dreamt of a man with a dog coming to see who we were and why we were there. This is the classic 'site guardian'. Later, immediately before waking up at sunrise, both of us experienced the same scene in our independent dreams. G was looking into a shop window. The interior was empty and dusty. In my dream, I and a friend who is closely associated with Carn Ingli were looking into a similarly neglected shop window, but I flourished the key and we were about to open the door with the intention of re-opening the shop for business.

Gospel Pass is where SS Peter and Paul are said to have preached. Could this really be? There was certainly great contact between the Silures tribe of South Wales and the Jews and early Christians. These links, including family ties, are explored in *The Drama of the Lost Disciples* by George Jowett. SS Peter and Paul were sheltered by the family of Caractacus in Rome. They may have come here in the late 50s AD. Much more likely, however, is an association with James the Just, brother of Jesus and holder of the title Joseph the Arimathea after the crucifixion. Read more about this in *Bloodline of the Holy Grail* by Laurence Gardner. The Roman Church would like to have swept all memory of Jesus' real family and its British links away, just as the final contents of the New Testament were highly selective. Unable to do so, it would have suited the religious authorities in the Middle Ages to have attributed such events as preaching in the first century at Gospel Pass to Paul, rather than James. The Celtic spiritual tradition is closer to that of James the brother of Jesus (and closer to that of St John the Divine) rather than

Looking north from Lord Hereford's Knob (The Twmpa), Powys

to that of Paul. Followers of the Way of Jesus did, no doubt, come this way very early in the Christian era.

The special spiritual nature of this place was recognised in the late 19th century. An Anglican deacon, Rev. Joseph Leycester Lyne, subsequently known as Father Ignatius, self-styled Evangelist Monk

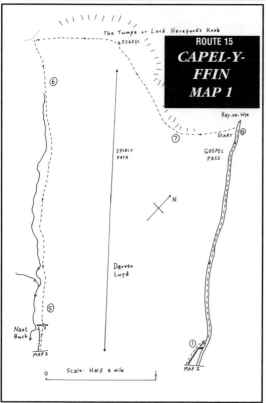

The Twmpa or Lord Hereford's Knob
▲2263ft

ROUTE 15
CAPEL-Y-FFIN
MAP 1

Hay-on-Wye

⑥

⑦ START ⑩

SPIRIT PATH

GOSPEL PASS

N

Darren Lwyd

⑤

Nant Bwch

MAP 2

Scale: Half a mile

0 ½

MAP 2

①

of the British Church, laid the foundation stone of his monastery at Capel-y-ffin in 1870. A famous orator, he raised funds through preaching tours. Out of favour with the Anglican authorities, he was ordained by a wandering prelate, styled by the Patriarch of Antioch, in 1898. Father Ignatius died at his sister's house in Surrey in 1908 and was buried in his monastery. His creation became a dependency of the Anglican Benedictine community of Caldey Island and was transferred with them to the Roman Catholic Church in 1913. The Roman Catholic convert, artist and craftsman, Eric Gill, lived here from 1924 to 1928. His practice of incest with his daughter was in contrast to the life-style of Father Ignatius, whom the Rev. Francis Kilvert recorded meeting in his famous diary, describing Father Ignatius as 'a man of gentle simple kind manners'.

Kilvert also described the little church at Capel-y-ffin (which means 'Chapel of the boundary' and is near where Gwent and Powys meet) as reminding him of an owl. Alfred Watkins noted in both *The Ley Hunter's Manual* and *The Old Straight Track* that its churchyard cross is on a ley. Watkins' ley went south-westwards to Pen y Gadair Fawr (and passing not too far away from the interestingly-named Blacksmith's Anvil, overlooking this sacred valley - where souls are hammered into shape?). This is at an angle of about 40 degrees, corresponding with the moonrise in northerly major standstill. When I dowsed here with G I was unaware of the moon alignments (I found out about them when a friend lent me a

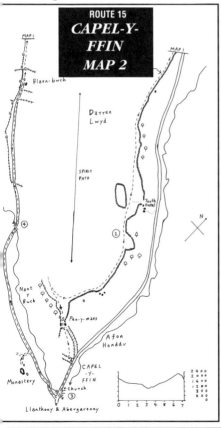

copy of *The First Stonehenge* by Gaynor Francis). My dowsing revealed the chief path to run through Capel-y-ffin's churchyard cross to the 2263ft summit of The Twmpa or Lord Hereford's Knob. This runs at an angle of 320 degrees which I now realise is the moonset in northerly major standstill.

The feminine aspect of Capel-y-ffin may explain visions of the Virgin Mary (the goddess if seen through eyes uncluttered by Christian dogma) seen here. The first appeared to four boys on August 30, 1880, around 8pm, in a field near the monastery. The same vision was seen on September 8 (the Feast of the Nativity of the

Blessed Virgin) and again a week later. A statue of the Virgin Mary has been erected on the spot of one of the visions. Were these earthlights (see *Earth Lights Revelations* by Paul Devereux)?

Route
(Mile 0) Go left from the car park, gradually descending with the road or walking on the moorland parallel to it. Reach a cattle grid and bear right from the road to walk with a wall on your left **(Mile 1)**.

Pass above Capel-y-ffin youth hostel (Mile 2) and keep the wall on your left until it turns left and the path bears right around the southern end of Darren Lwyd. Turn sharply left down a path coming up from your left and descend to pass the buildings of Pen-y-maes. Go ahead over a stile to take the fieldpath down to the road and bear right to the church at Capel-y-ffin **(Mile 3)**.

Cross the bridge over Nant y Bwch and turn right up a lane which passes the monastery on your left. Continue up this lane, crossing Nant y Bwch again **(Mile 4)** and reaching Blaen-bwch. Go ahead along what is now a mountain track, keeping the stream below on your left **(Mile 5)**.

Climb beyond the source of the stream **(Mile 6)** to the mountain ridge. Go right to attain the 2263ft summit of the Twmpa or Lord Hereford's Knob. Descend with the clear path down to the car park beside the road in Gospel Pass **(7 miles)**.

Distance:	4¼ miles
Start:	Car park at Llanthony Priory, grid ref.: SO 288278
OS Map:	Outdoor Leisure 13 (Brecon Beacons - East), Landranger 161 (Abergavenny & the Black Mountains)
Public Transport:	None. Take a taxi from the nearest railway station at Abergavenny. The nearest bus stop (no. 20 Abergavenny - Hereford, tel. 01633 266336) is six miles away at Llanvihangel Crucorney.

Introduction

Llanthony is derived from Llanddewi Nant Honddu (Church of St David on the River Honddu) and is the site of St David's first hermitage. Obviously a place of great spiritual power, it can be perceived as both heaven and hell. Its isolated, mountain-locked darkness is captured by Phil Rickman in his novel *December*. When Giraldus Cambrensis came this way in 1188, he noted that here 'is a site most suited to the practice of religion and better chosen for canonical discipline than that of any of the other monasteries in the whole Island of Britain'.

The priory was erected after William de Lacy, a knight in the service of Hugh de Lacy, came across the ruins of St David's cell in the early 12th century. Deciding to abandon worldly pursuits and spend the rest of his days in contemplation here, he attracted other hermits, notably Ernisius, who had been chaplain to Queen Matilda, the wife of Henry I. A new church was built and the community became a house of Augustinian canons, otherwise known as Black Canons. Nationalist stirrings amongst the Welsh led to the canons retreating to a safe haven in Gloucester in 1135 and the mother house at Llanthony was soon stripped bare to furnish it. New funds resulting from the English invasion of Ireland led to a fine building being erected from about 1175, with the work completed by 1230.

Just four canons needed to be pensioned off when the Dissolution finally came into effect in the Vale of Ewyas in 1538.

The ruined priory eventually came into the hands of Walter Savage Landor, a contemporary of Wordsworth, Coleridge, Shelley

Llanthony Priory

and Byron. Landor had an epic poem called *Gebir* published in 1798 and also wrote *Imaginary Conversations* between historical figures such as Dante and Beatrice. He bought the Llanthony estate in 1808 and aspired to be a model owner, planting trees and improving roads. He planned to build a mansion in the woods overlooking the priory, right next to the line of the ley or spirit path. The ruin of Siarpal is all that remains of that idea now. Frittering away his fortune, Landor became disenchanted with the place, stating that he could never be happy there, or comfortable, or at peace. The 'very features of the country' became too much for him. He came to 'hate and detest' them. He left in 1813 and died in Florence in 1864.

Having gauged the power of the spirit, for good or ill, at Llanthony, its significance to ley hunters is also strong, as witnessed by the cover picture of *Lines on the Landscape* by Nigel Pennick and Paul Devereux. This depicts an ancient straight track climbing the hillside to the opposite side of the valley from Llanthony Priory. This marks a ley which was known to Alfred Watkins. Photographs of it feature in *The Old Straight Track* (figures 75 and 76), showing the line sighted through the chancel of the original abbey at an angle of 16 degrees (20-4 for magnetic variation).

The ley is sighted northwards to a notch on the ridge. Watkins used sighting staves to indicate the lines of his leys, like the original ley-men or dodmen. The wand or staff is an ancient symbol of authority. It was at Llanthony while 'idly watching a snail ... with his horns advanced' that 'it came as a flash' to Watkins 'that he was called the dodman because he carried the two sighting staves on his head'. The use of such staves required much 'dodging or doddering' before they marked a final position. Men of skill and knowledge did this surveying in ancient times, hence the status of their staves. An obsolete meaning of a 'rod' is 'a path, a way, a road'. The figure of the Long Man of Wilmington with his two staffs, carved on the Sussex Downs, springs to mind.

Route

Walking back from the car park **(Mile 0)**, pass St David's Church on your left and the ruined priory and the Abbey Hotel on your right. Cross a waymarked stile beside a gate and go right to walk with a wall on your right to a second stile beside a gate. Go ahead over this and walk away from the priory up a track. Leave this track at a stream, bearing left as waymarked by a yellow arrow. Continue over a third stile beside a gate and climb to a fourth stile. Bear left uphill to the top of woodland, cross two stiles in successive fences and reach a waymark post. Go right to come to a gate. Continue with conifer trees on your left. Don't be misled by the next yellow waymark arrow, which is pointing back the way you've come. At the end of the conifer trees on your left, turn right downhill to a stile beside a gate. Cross this and the next stile, above a gate to its right.

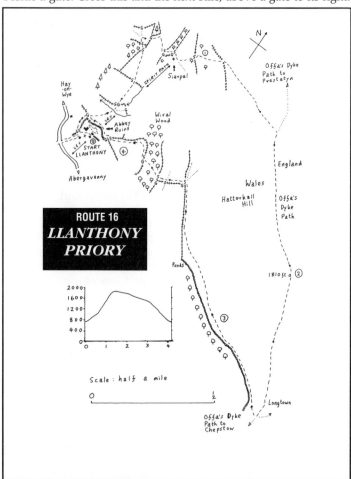

ROUTE 16

LLANTHONY PRIORY

Scale: half a mile

The ruin of Siarpal is on your right. The ley crosses the track some 15 yards after the ruin of Siarpal and heads down to the priory. Turn left uphill, as waymarked by a yellow arrow. Cross a stile in a fence and bear right as you climb **(Mile 1)**.

This steep path crosses the remains of an old wall. Keep climbing to the ridge and the Offa's Dyke Path. Turn right along this nationaltrail to overlook England (Herefordshire) on your left. Pass a trig point at 1810 feet above sea level **(Mile 2)**.

Descend to a track junction. Turn sharply right to descend with a track that is soon joined by a wall coming up from your left. Continue along this when it keeps above the wall **(Mile 3)**.

Descend gradually to be joined by a fence on your left. Look out for a signposted junction. Turn left at it to cross a stile and go downhill to take another stile into woodland. Bear right with the woodland track, emerge over a stile beside a gate and go right to follow the edge of this field, turning left in the corner **(Mile 4)** and taking a stile in the bottom right-hand corner. Walk with the priory wall on your left and retrace your steps to the car park.

Distance:	10¼ miles
Start:	Bus stop in Beaufort Street, Crickhowell, grid ref.: SO 218184
Finish:	Bus station, Abergavenny, grid ref.: SO 301140
OS Maps:	Outdoor Leisure 13 (Brecon Beacons East), Landranger 161 (Abergavenny)
Public Transport:	Bus no. 21 (Brecon - Abergavenny - Pontypool - Cwmbran - Newport) links the two ends of this linear walk, tel. 01633 266336 for details. Beacons Bus no. 29 runs from Abergavenny to Crickhowell (and on to Brecon) on summer Sundays and Bank Holiday Mondays (tel. 01874 623156). Trains run to Abergavenny (on the Newport - Shrewsbury line, tel. 0345 484950).

Introduction

This is a strange tale. Rosetta Reinke is an American lady who knew nothing of Wales, although she does have some Welsh blood coursing through her veins, until she was moved by powerful dreams to travel here in search of St Keyne's tomb. This beautiful daughter of Brychan ended her days as a hermit at Llangenny, near Crickhowell, where the church is dedicated to her (n.b. Cenau is an alternative spelling of Keyne).

Legend tells how on the day of her death a column of fire was seen standing above St Keyne's cell and two angels descended to where she lay on branches on the floor. One removed her sack-cloth habit, vested her in a sheet of linen and a crimson tunic, then cast over her a mantle embroidered with gold, saying 'Come with us and we will lead you to the Kingdom of Your Father'. St Keyne died on October 8, now her saint's day, and was buried in her oratory by her nephew St Cattwg (Cadoc - Sir Galahad?). She left behind a prophecy, recorded by Chris Barber in *More Mysterious Wales*, that her tomb would 'lie a long time unknown, until the coming of other people, who by my prayers I shall bring hither. Them I will protect and defend, and in this place shall the name of the Lord be blessed forever'.

The location of her tomb has been lost for centuries. We do have what is believed to be St Keyne's bell, however. It was found by a farmer shortly after he demolished an old building said to have been her oratory around 1790. This is believed to have stood at about grid ref. SO 241181 above the private drive to Pendarren House, Llangenny. Nearby is a spring (or a muddy patch!) which can be taken to be the saint's well. The first of a newly-wed couple to drink from this well would be 'master' throughout their married life. A similar tale is told of St Keyne's Well near Liskeard in Cornwall. When the bridegroom dashed to be first at the well after the marriage ceremony, he found his effort was in vain because the bride had brought a bottle of its water to the church! St Keyne appears to have been a woman who liked to 'wear the trousers'.

In *The Glastonbury Zodiac*, a book which the author Mary Caine (a descendant of William Blake) dedicates to St Keyne, the connection is made between St Keyne and the goddess Ceridwen, the British Ceres and Old Mother Cary. No wonder she spent so much of her life in the horn of Cornwall - the cornucopia of Ceres-Ceridwen-Cary-Kerin-Keyne. This harvest goddess is also the golden horn of Capricorn the White Hart and Unicorn, the Golden Hind of December where Kerin's seeds are stored in winter. This is the Ceryneian Hind that was captured by the dragon and which evaded Hercules for a whole year. The name of the pub in Llangenny is the Dragon's Head, while nearby is the Golden Grove complete with a standing stone.

A logical explanation for the site of St Keyne's tomb would be the oratory that was demolished in 1790, near the holy well. Why, then, the legend of it being lost until found again by 'other people'? All this was unknown to me until Rosetta Reinke wrote from America, having read my book *In the Footsteps of King Arthur*, in which I mention dreaming on Carn Ingli. Rosetta knew that St Brynach, who dreamt on Carn Ingli, was a brother-in-law of Keyne and just felt she had to find out more about the dreaming project. She flew across the Atlantic to dream with me on Carn Ingli in early October, 1997.

Rosetta's involvement with St Keyne began decades ago when she was pregnant with her daughter, Kendra. She had a powerful, vivid, dream of the sort that is impossible to dismiss or forget. It led to her giving her daughter the name Kendra and to Rosetta investigating the life of St Keyne. Eventually, her daughter grew up and Rosetta was free to pursue her interest in this faraway Celtic saint. This involved putting her bookshop up for sale in order to raise funds for transatlantic trips. Rosetta was guided to meet Mary Caine and then found me. Her goal was the discovery of St Keyne's lost tomb. At the time, my own quest was leading towards the truth of the Battle of Camlan, King Arthur's last battle, in particular who fought alongside Derfel Gadarn and who, with him, guarded the Holy Grail. As a result of our meeting, I realised how St Cadoc was Sir Galahad and had been an ally of Derfel in a previous life, so Rosetta knew that she was the reincarnation of St Gwladys, the elder sister of St Keyne (and the mother of St Cadoc).

After asking the goddess of Carn Ingli for success with her quest, Rosetta was driven to the Llangenny area by her husband, complete with maps and guidebooks to find places connected with St Keyne. On the very last day of her trip, on October 8 (St Keyne's Day), she was led by psychic intuition to a mound on the western slope of the Sugar Loaf at grid ref. SO 244186, near a farmhouse called Ty Mawr. Unable to stay and enquire about it, Rosetta sent me pictures and requested my help. Not knowing the Crickhowell area and without the funds to travel even to the southern part of Powys, this was confined to work in the library. I had no idea what to expect when Rosetta was able to make a surprise trip back to Wales in late February, 1998. Before checking in to our hotel in Crickhowell, Rosetta drove me to see some local standing stones.

I felt moved by a very powerful standing stone just above the Great Oak Road, between Crickhowell and Llangenny. It is important to emphasise that I knew nothing about this stone, this area or, even, the direction I was facing (it was a dull, cloudy, day). I have since read about this Great Oak Standing Stone in *The Ancient Stones of Wales* by Chris Barber and J.G. Williams. Read this book yourself to find out what happened when J.G. Williams was filmed by BBC Wales here!

Asking my dowsing rods to show me the direction of St Keyne's tomb when at the Great Oak Standing Stone, they pointed me in an easterly direction, about 86 degrees (90-4 for magnetic variation). I did not realise this was east until I took out my compass. I didn't know where I was (grid ref. SO 223185) let alone the locations of any other places (such as Llangenny and the Sugar Loaf). I could see down the line I had dowsed that going in its opposite, westward, direction, it led to the church with its distinctive spire down in Crickhowell.

The 1955ft summit of the Sugar Loaf above Abergavenny

Only later, in our hotel room, did I unfold what was an unfamiliar map and draw the line I had dowsed. Only then, too, did Rosetta show me her map with the location of the mound she had been led to the previous St Keyne's Day. I hadn't known its exact location until then. I hadn't even bothered to look for it, not being furnished with its grid reference. I had read more about SS Keyne, Gwladys, Gwynlliw and Cadoc in the library and intended to ask Chris Barber for help when down his way in the spring of 1998. The line I had dowsed led straight over the spot where Rosetta had been led! It is moments like this (and they are oh, so typical of this quest) that are unforgettable.

Rosetta had not dowsed at the Great Oak Standing Stone for the direction of St Keyne's tomb as I had. Her methods are different. She had asked her husband to drive her around and follow where intuition told her to go. With time running out, this had led them to the road running south to Llangenny at grid ref. SO 239186, which happens to be where the line I had dowsed (my spirit path) crosses that road. Stopping the car, she had looked across the valley and, with binoculars, identified a mound in the correct place, where she felt sure St Keyne was buried. There is nothing in guidebook or on map to indicate a burial mound at this spot. There was nobody in Ty Mawr to help Rosetta when she drove to it and had time merely to photograph this mound before hastening to Heathrow airport.

So, we went next day to the mound near Ty Mawr. It is clearly not an ancient burial mound. There was a small quarry here and this is its spoil heap. Nevertheless, we both, using our different methods, were sure that this is the site of St Keyne's tomb. It is a good position for a saint to choose, on the side of a holy hill facing west, where the sun sets at the equinoxes. The quarrying has meant that we'll never be sure, but I felt that there had been a cave here, facing the sunset, that St Keyne used. Perhaps her burial mound lies under the spoil heap. Look at the OS map for yourself to see that this site is on the line of a spirit path leading east from the church in Crickhowell, through the standing stone in Great Oak Road, past an earthwork at grid ref. SO 228186, over the supposed tomb of St Keyne and on to the summit of Sugar Loaf.

The sacred nature of the 1995ft peak of the Sugar Loaf was recognised by Alfred Watkins. In *The Old Straight Track*, he noted that a ley ran slightly north of east from Sugar Loaf to Garway Hill by way of Bryn Arw and Llanvihangel Crucorney, with another ley running very slightly south of east from Sugar Loaf to Ysgyryd Fawr.

The parish church in Crickhowell is, surprisingly, dedicated to an East Anglian saint, Blessed Saint Edmund, King, Martyr and Virgin. Built in the last years of the 13th century by Lady Sybil Pauncefote, it houses an effigy of her without hands. These were demanded as ransom when her husband was captured by infidels.

Abergavenny Castle, near the other end of this walk, also has a gruesome, bloody tale. This is where Welsh chieftains were massacred as defenceless guests by Normans at a Christmas feast in 1175.

Route

(Mile 0) Go to the square in the centre of Crickhowell and, with the Bear Hotel across the road on your right, turn left along High Street. Very soon, take a narrow passage on your right known as Silver Lane. This leads to Church Lane and you'll see the church on your left. Retrace your steps to the square and this time go straight ahead to leave the Bear Hotel on your left and follow Standard Street. Pass Greenhill Way on your right. Turn left along Great Oak Road and take a gate in the hedge on your right to see the Great Oak Standing Stone. Retrace your steps along Great Oak Road and turn left to resume your previous direction,

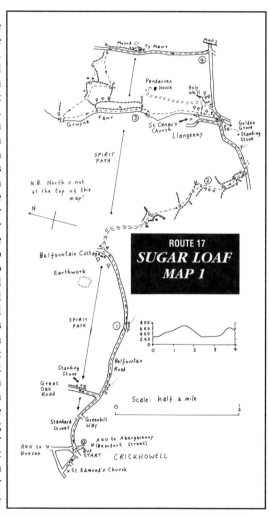

ROUTE 17
SUGAR LOAF
MAP 1

Scale: half a mile

climbing with Belfountain Road **(Mile 1)**.

Reach Belfountain Cottage and turn right along an access lane. When this reaches farm buildings, fork left to walk with a wall on your right and cross a stile beside a gate in the corner. Bear right to cut across the next field to take a gate in its right-hand corner ahead, continue beside a fence on your right, turn right through a gate in this and turn left to reach a gate at the end of a lower fence on your right **(Mile 2)**.

Descend to a road and go left downhill towards Llangenny. Take a signposted path on your right to divert to the Golden Grove standing stone. Return to the road and pass the bridge on your right to go ahead past the Dragon Head Inn on your left and reach St Cenau's Church, Llangenny. Retrace your steps to the bridge and turn left to cross it this time. Bear left to start climbing uphill but soon bear left over a stile to follow the signposted path which goes upstream with the river, Grwyne Fawr, on your left **(Mile 3)**.

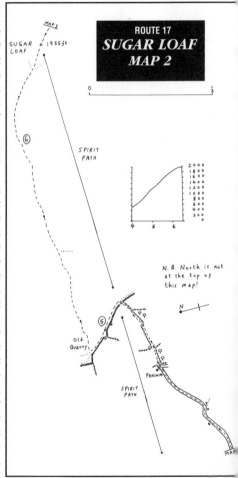

ROUTE 17
SUGAR LOAF
MAP 2

N. B. North is not at the top of this map!

After passing two private footbridges spanning the river on your left, reach a third footbridge which is used by a public footpath. Do not cross it! Turn sharply right to follow a path up the hillside towards the farm buildings of Ty-draw. The OS map shows the right of way going through this farmyard, but the lady of the house requested that I turned right just before it to walk with a fence on my left to a gate in the corner through which I turned to bear left back up to the public footpath (thus avoiding the farmyard). Follow the path to a road and go right. Pass the supposed site of St Keyne's tomb just before a farmhouse on your left **(Mile 4)**.

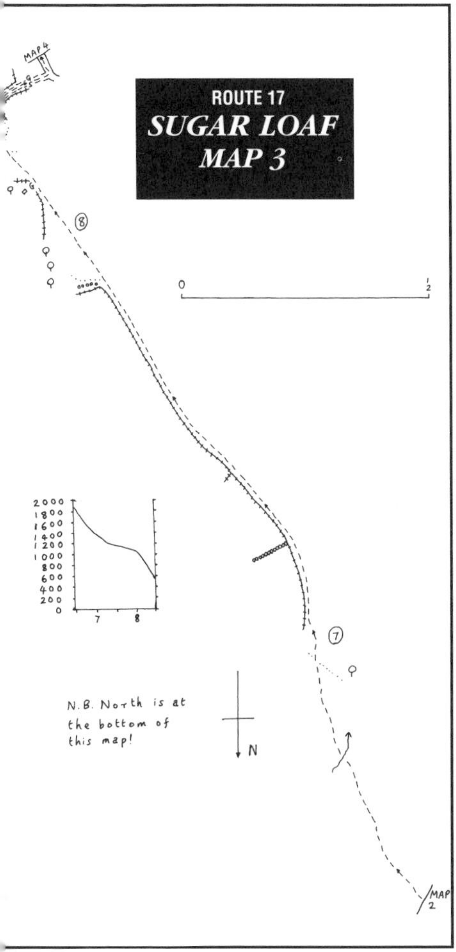

Turn left at a road junction and climb to a house called Pencwm on your left. The road makes a sharp turn to the right here. Leave it by taking a gate ahead at the bend and walking with woodland behind the fence on your right. Take the right-hand of two gates ahead and keep climbing, this time with a fence on your left. Continue through a small gate to put the fence back on your right

ROUTE 17
SUGAR LOAF
MAP 3

0   ½

2000
1800
1600
1400
1200
1000
800
600
400
200
0

7   8

N.B. North is at the bottom of this map!

N

and climb to a gate giving access to open moorland. This gate also happens to mark where the spirit path crosses the mountain wall towards the open summit of the Sugar Loaf **(Mile 5)**.

Go left to walk with the mountain wall on your left. Pass a gate in it, then a second gate in a recess. When the wall turns left, turn right to walk past an old quarry on your left as you follow a path away from the wall to the summit of Sugar Loaf **(Mile 6)**. Bear right when descending, cross a stream and reach a fence on your left **(Mile 7)**. Continue with this fence on your left for one mile **(Mile 8)**. When the fence and a broken wall turn left, go straight ahead to descend to a gate in the far bottom-left corner. Take this to reach a lane and go right to a junction with a road. Turn left to reach where this road bends left. Leave it by bearing right at this bend over a stile beside a gate and following the signposted path

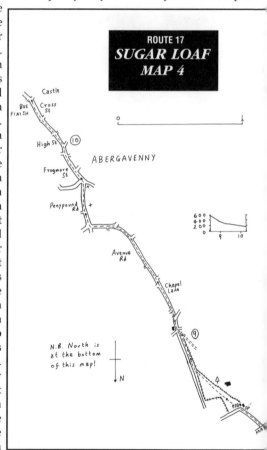

ROUTE 17
**SUGAR LOAF
MAP 4**

Castle
Bus FINISH
Cross St
High St
ABERGAVENNY
Frogmore St
Penypound Rd
Avenue Rd
Chapel Lane

N.B. North is at the bottom of this map!

↓N

to a stile in the far, pointed, corner ahead. Go ahead along an enclosed path which runs parallel to and above a road on your left **(Mile 9)**.

Go straight ahead at a crossroads, but when the road starts to bend right, turn left through a gate and reach Chapel Lane. Go ahead, passing Chain Close on your left, then Chapel Orchard on your left, Linden Avenue on your right and Avenue Crescent on your left. Proceed down Avenue Road, passing Harold Road and

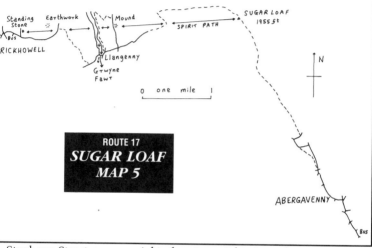

Stanhope Street on your right, then turn right along the pavement of Penypound Road into the centre of Abergavenny. Follow Frogmore Street to the High Street, then Cross Street **(Mile 10)**. Reach the bus station on your left. The railway station is further ahead on your left (it is signposted), while you should turn right along Lower Castle Street if visiting the castle before descending to the bus station.

Distance:	13¼ miles
Start:	Whitland railway station, grid ref.: SN 199165
Finish:	Narberth railway station grid ref.: SN 120147
OS Maps:	Outdoor Leisure 36 (South Pembrokeshire), and Explorer 177, Landranger 158 (Tenby)
Public Transport:	Trains link the two railway stations at the ends of this linear walk (tel. 0345 484950 for details)

Introduction

It was at Arberth (Narberth) that Pwyll, Prince of Dyfed, held his chief court in the dim and distant past recorded in *The Mabinogion.* Pwyll went to the top of a mound above the court, called Gorsedd Arberth, to 'see a wonder'. This was none other than the goddess Rhiannon on her white horse. The ruins of the castle at the end of this walk date from after a successful Welsh attack on a Norman castle in 1257. The mound at the northern end (near the road) may be prehistoric, however. Is this the very mound resorted to by Pwyll?

Watch the sunset from the mound and you'll notice the nearby church tower. A dreamer on Carn Ingli dreamt of an entrance to a tunnel that emerged on this mound with this very view of the church tower, confirming that it was Narberth. Knowing that tunnel legends can be folk memories of leys or spirit paths, I enquired of locals, including a lady in Narberth's Wilson Museum. Narberth has, it seems, several tunnel legends (suggesting that it is a focal point for leys, as would only be expected with an ancient capital). One particularly interesting 'tunnel' was said to link Narberth with Whitland Abbey. With both towns connected by the railway which branches off the main line at Whitland and terminates at Pembroke Dock after visiting Tenby, here was a convenient route for a linear walk served by trains at both ends.

So, I headed for the tranquil ruins of Whitland Abbey, founded by the Cistercians just north of Whitland in 1151. I don't know if this was a sacred site already, but Cistercians seemed to have a nose for such places, while a Roman road passed nearby on its way west from Carmarthen. There isn't much to see at the site of the abbey

The east end of the ruined Whitland Abbey, looking along the ley to the altar

now, but it was easy to identify where the altar used to stand. This was where I meditated for a couple of hours before taking out my dowsing rods and asking them to show me any spirit path to Narberth castle mound.

Holding the thought of a shining path and a vision of Narberth castle mound in my head, I walked around the site of the altar. This isn't my usual practice as I had come with the fixed idea of walking what seemed an attractive line to Narberth (a great excuse for a delightful walk, partly along a section of the waymarked Landsker Borderlands Trail). Normally I would ask to be shown the primary ley or most important spirit path at such a place, then follow wherever my dowsing rods led me.

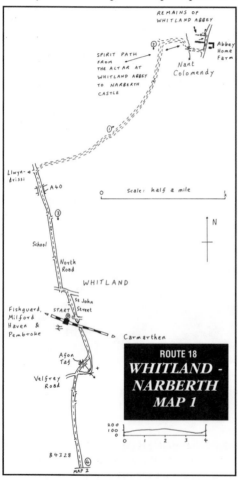

REMAINS OF
WHITLAND ABBEY

SPIRIT PATH
FROM
THE ALTAR AT
WHITLAND ABBEY
TO NARBERTH
CASTLE

Abbey
Home
Farm

Nant
Colomendy

Llwyn-
drissi

A40

Scale: half a mile

School

North
Road

WHITLAND

St John
Street

Fishguard,
Milford
Haven &
Pembroke

START

Carmarthen

Afon
Taf

Velfrey
Road

ROUTE 18
WHITLAND -
NARBERTH
MAP 1

200
100
0

B 4328

MAP 2

My dowsing rods indicated a line which the compass revealed as running through the altar at an angle of 70 degrees (74-4 for magnetic variation). Extending this line, whose angle might suggest a link with sunrise around Beltane (early May) and Lughnassadh (early August), west-south-west brings it to the castle mound in Narberth. I did not measure the required angle beforehand and I was not aware of the angle, not even thinking of the general direction, that I needed to dowse! I simply concentrated on 'tuning-in' and this was the result. Discovering that I had dowsed the desired line was pleasing.

This spirit path crosses the walking route a couple of times and further satisfaction comes from confirming this by dowsing. The spirit path happens to go through the offices of SPARC (South Pembrokeshire Partnership for Action with Rural Communities), the agency responsible for the waymarking and 'footpath furniture' (stiles, gates, footbridges, signposts etc) along this walk, as it enters Narberth. As well as the castle ruins, make sure you visit Narberth's Landsker Visitor Centre, which includes an interpretation of *The Mabinogion,* and the Wilson Museum, which houses a fascinating collection of local memorabilia.

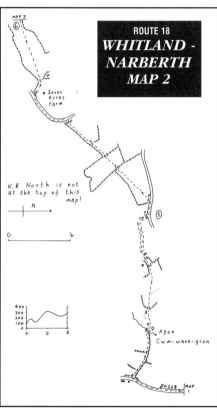

**ROUTE 18
WHITLAND -
NARBERTH
MAP 2**

Whitland was a royal residence too and was where a great assembly met to codify Welsh laws during the reign of Hywell Dda (the Good) in the first half of the 10th century. Find out more about him in Whitland's Hywell Dda exhibition, near the start of this walk, off St Mary's Street, running east from St John Street near the railway level crossing in Whitland.

Route

(Mile 0) With your back to Whitland railway station, go right and turn left along St John Street away from the level crossing. Turn left at the end of the street and turn right at North Road. Take a bridge over the A40 and turn right with a signposted by-way for Whitland Abbey **(Mile 1).** Turn right when this track comes to a T junction. Cross a footbridge beside a ford. Reach a road and go left to a signposted path through a

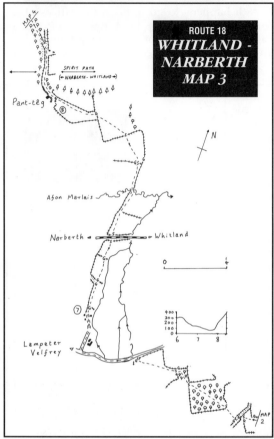

ROUTE 18
WHITLAND - NARBERTH
MAP 3

gate. Take this to a gate on your left giving access to the abbey ruins. Retrace your steps **(Miles 2 and 3)** to Whitland railway station.

Take the B4328 road south, out of Whitland, taking the level crossing carefully. Bear right with the new road to take a bridge over the River Taf and pass Velfrey Road on your right **(Mile 4)**. Reach a Landsker Borderlands Trail waymark post on your right and turn right through a kissing-gate to follow the right-hand edges of three fields to a footbridge. Cross this and climb with a waymarked path through scrubby woodland. Bear right along a track and pass gorse bushes.

Leave the track when it bears right. Go straight ahead to a ladder-stile giving access to a hedged path. Follow a farm access track to a road **(Mile 5)**. Go left along this road for 100 yards, then bear left with a signposted path. Continue over a series of stiles and along the left-hand edges of three fields to another road. Bear left and pass Seven Acres Farm on your right.

Turn right with the Landsker Borderlands Trail through a kissing-gate. After 100 yards, turn left over a stone stile and continue **(Mile 6)** to a stile beside a gate in the far corner which gives access to an old green lane. Turn left along this, cross another stile beside a gate and turn right to reach the corner of woodland where a stile invites you to follow a path which emerges over a stile in the wood's bottom corner. Go right to descend to take the left-hand of two gates and go ahead to join a road. Bear left along this for 400 yards.

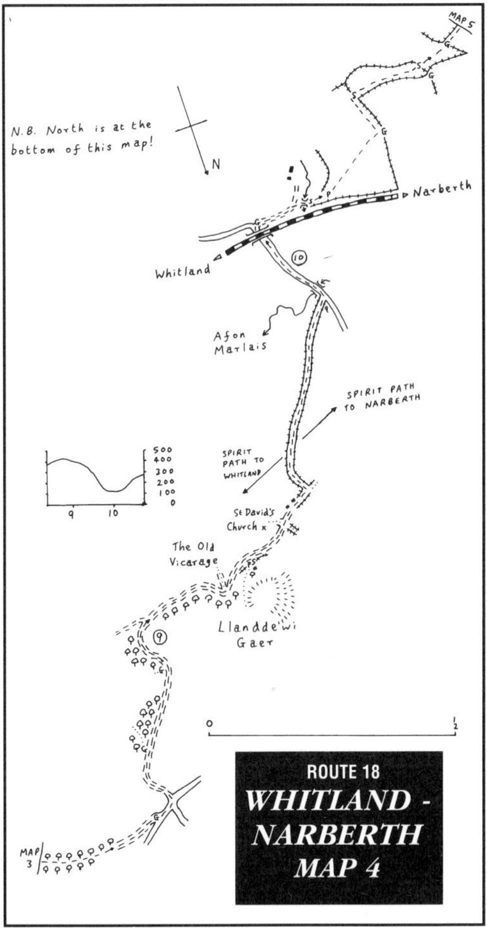
MAP 5
N.B. North is at the bottom of this map!
N
Narberth
Whitland
10
Afon Marlais
SPIRIT PATH TO NARBERTH
SPIRIT PATH TO WHITLAND
500
400
300
200
100
0
9
10
St David's Church
The Old Vicarage
Llanddewi Gaer
9
0
½
MAP 3

ROUTE 18
WHITLAND - NARBERTH MAP 4

Turn right down the lane for White House Mill trout fishery. Continue with a track **(Mile 7)** until it bears left. Go straight ahead here to cross the railway line. Go ahead and bear left over a footbridge. Continue along the right-hand edge of the next field to cross a stile beside a gate in the corner. Follow the path which gradually bears left to the buildings of Pant-teg **(Mile 8)**. Go right up its access track. The spirit path crosses this track shortly after you pass a corner of a field on your right.

Bear left at a fork. Converge with a track coming from your left and go ahead to join a road. Turn left to a crossroads where you take the access lane which is signposted for St David's Church. Descend to pass a memorial bench to Jane O'Neil **(Mile 9)**. Pass a track for the old vicarage on your left. A signposted path on your right offers a diversion to climb to the hillfort of Llanddewi Gaer. Pass above St David's Church on your left. Continue past Lane End studio and gallery.

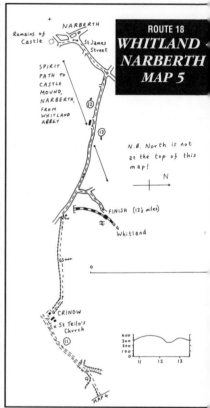

Turn left down a muddy, hedged, track (which is crossed by the spirit path shortly after the track has bent right). Go left at a road **(Mile 10)** and pass under a railway bridge, immediately after which, on your right, is an old holy well (Ffynnon Claf).

Turn right along a signposted track. As this bears left, turn right to cross a footbridge and follow the right-hand edge of a small field. Bear left at a signpost to climb to a waymark post near a gate. Go left to walk with a fence on your right until you reach a stile in it. Turn right to cross this and continue over a stone stile at the far end of this field.

Cut across another field to take a gateway and go ahead along the left-hand edge of the next field to reach a lane. Bear left along this and pass **(Mile 11)** St Teilo's Church, Crinow, on your right.

Turn right with the signposted path past the buildings of Crinow Farm, climbing, then turning right, as waymarked. Take an old green lane on your left and continue with a hedge on your left to reach a road. Go right. If you wish to go straight to Narberth railway station, turn right and turn right again. If proceeding into Narberth, go ahead to pass the headquarters of SPARC (South Pembrokeshire Partnership for Action with Rural Communities) in an old school on your left. This happens to be on the spirit path. Turn left down St James Street. Fork left to pass Narberth's Wilson Museum on your right and descend to the castle ruins. Retrace your steps for the turning to Narberth railway station.

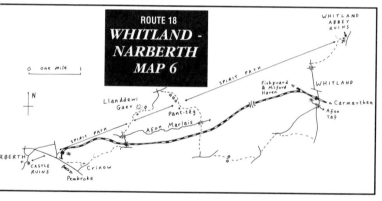

Distance:	5¼ miles
Start:	Burry Port railway station, grid ref.: SN 447007
OS Maps:	Explorer 10 to be re-numbered 164 (Gower), Landranger 159 (Swansea)
Public Transport:	Trains run to Burry Port from Swansea and Carmarthen (tel. 0345 484950)

Introduction

Nature has reclaimed the valley of the Nant Dyfatty from the coalmines that were served by the railway whose course is followed at the start of this walk. The local members of the Ramblers' Association have also done sterling work regaining and maintaining public access to this countryside. Their work involved the restoration of a path which has long been known locally as a Coffin Trail.

The nature of this landscape forces it to take a winding route south from the road junction at grid ref. SN 450035 on Mynydd Pen-bre to Capel Carmel at grid ref. SO 458022. This includes a sharp left turn and a steep climb at the end. Although the physical path has to follow the contours, it aims at a chapel which is at the southern end of a straight spirit path which coincides with the initial straight section of the south-bound Coffin Trail (before it turns to go through the farmyard of Rhiwlas - now avoided by a new path diversion). The spirit path is terrain-oblivious and the physical Coffin Trail is linked to it.

Where the spirit path enters the northern end of the wood below Mynydd Pen-bre, three miners were drowned when they hit an underground lake while working in an incline. The mine was never used again.

In flatter, gentler landscapes, the coffin trails, corpse paths, spirit ways, church walks or whatever name employed can run straight, or nearly as straight as the spirit paths they reflect. John Palmer's research on *Doodwegen* (Death Roads) in the Netherlands is quoted in Paul Devereux's book *Shamanism and the Mystery Lines,* while the final chapter of *Lines on the Landscape,* by Nigel Pennick and Paul Devereux, links leys, spirit paths and coffin trails.

When making our final journeys, it seems that it is important to try and conform to an ideal of straightness, no doubt in the hope of reaching our desired destination quickly and easily. As Chapter 3, Verse 4 of Luke's gospel exhorts: 'Prepare ye the way of the Lord, make his paths straight'.

Route

(Mile 0) With your back to the railway station, go right along Station Road. Turn left immediately before the Bristol Hotel to take the course of the old Cwm Capel Branch of the Gwendraeth Valley Railway (now a metalled path). Continue across a road to pass the Pemberton Arms on your left. Bear right at Nant y Felin, cross a bridge over the stream (Nant Dafatty) and bear right up a slope. Go right along a lane, soon passing an old chimney on your right and a quarry on your left **(Mile 1)**.

Pass two turnings on your left before bearing left at a fork. Fork left from an access track to a house on your right and climb to a gate. Continue along the top of a wooded slope. Take a gate in a corner ahead on your left at the end of the woodland. Follow the path around the right side of a field and turn left in its corner. Turn right in the next corner to follow a hedged track taken by the Coffin Trail **(Mile 2)**.

When the Coffin Trail bears right towards Rhiwlas farm, take the waymarked gate ahead at this corner to walk along the left side of a field to reach a road. Turn right along the road. Reach the northern end of the Coffin Trail and turn right along its initial section, aiming dead straight for Capel Carmel. Bear left at a fork. Reach a house on your right and turn left through a kissing-gate. Go ahead through two more such gates and maintain your direction along a lane. Turn right through another kissing-gate and follow the left sides of three fields to reach the farm of Emlych **(Mile 3)**.

Turn right along an enclosed track which passes the farmhouse of Emlych on your right. Emerge through a kissing-gate to descend to the wooded floor of the valley, where you go left to walk along an old tramway. Turn left when you reach a road and climb to Capel Carmel. Retrace your steps down the road **(Mile 4)**.

Continue down the valley to bear left, as signposted, to return over the stream and along the course of the dismantled railway back to Burry Port **(Mile 5)**.

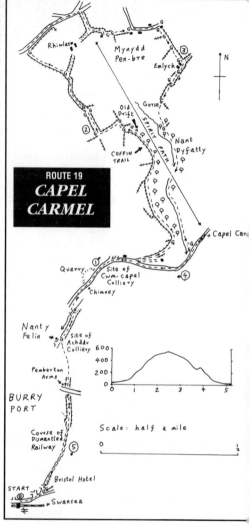

ROUTE 19

CAPEL CARMEL

Rhiwlas

Mynydd Pen-bre

Emlych

Old Drift

Gorse

Spirit Path

Nant Dyfatty

COFFIN TRAIL

+ Capel Car

Quarry

Site of Cwm-capel Colliery

Chimney

Nanty Felin

Site of Achddu Colliery

600
400
200
0

Pemberton Arms

BURRY PORT

Course of Dismantled Railway

Scale: half a mile

0   ½

Bristol Hotel

START

Swansea

Distance:	7 miles
Start:	Pengam railway station, grid ref.: ST 150975
OS Maps:	Explorer 166 (Rhondda & Merthyr Tydfil), Landranger 171 (Cardiff & Newport)
Public Transport:	Trains run to Pengam from Cardiff and Rhymney (tel. 0345 484950). Bus X38 runs from Cardiff to Bargoed via Gelligaer, Pen-pedair-heol and Pengam (tel. 01633 266336).

Introduction

That great hymn-writer the Rev. Sabine Baring-Gould reckoned that St Cattwg or Cadoc was the original of Sir Galahad. According to the Welsh Triads, Cadoc was one of the 'three knights of upright judgement' at King Arthur's court and one of the 'three knights that kept the Holy Grail'.

Cadoc's father was Gwynllyw (St Woolos), a neighbouring king to Arthur and notorious for his carnal desires and so, as the father of Sir Galahad, his pure son Cadoc, a prime candidate for the role of Sir Lancelot. Cadoc's mother was St Gwladys, who lived separately from her husband near the end of her life, including a spell at the windswept chapel that bears her name and is visited on this walk. St Gwladys was one of Brychan of Brycheiniog's 24 daughters (plus a reputed 12 sons from three wives). She had been carried off by Gwynllyw when a maiden because of her beauty and gentleness and when her father attempted to rescue her, King Arthur intervened on Gwynllyw's behalf.

A Celtic cross now marks the site of Capel Gwladys. Gelligaer's parish church is dedicated to her son St Cattwg (Cadoc). Nearby is the site of a Roman fort, with just low banks and ditches to remind us of this fort which stood on the Roman road between Brecon and Cardiff. Unlike most other auxiliary forts, it was built of stone from the first. The 500 men housed here practised erecting small marching camps on Gelligaer Common.

Examine the cup markings on the recumbent stone known as Maen Cattwg. Theories about these range from primitive maps of local sacred mounds, patterns of constellations in the sky to direction indicators of prehistoric trackways. Dowsing at this stone revealed the most important spirit path to go through it at an angle of 60 degrees, conforming to the alignment of Moonrise in northerly minor standstill.

Capel Gwladys

The path up to Capel Gwladys roughly followed another spirit path, dowsed as coming from Pen-pedair-heol (a name redolent of crossroads) at an angle of about 315 degrees. Is this linked to the Moonset in northerly major standstill (320 degrees) or to the sunset at the summer solstice (310 degrees)? Perhaps there are two lines.

Route
(Mile 0) Go left from Pengam railway station to join the B4254 and turn left to pass under the railway bridge. Climb with the pavement of this road to Pen-pedair-heol (or take bus X38). Reach the football

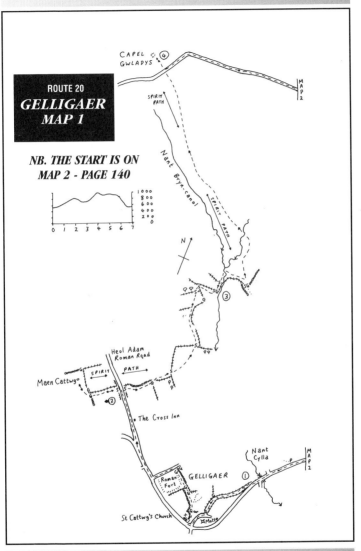

ROUTE 20
GELLIGAER
MAP 1

NB. THE START IS ON
MAP 2 - PAGE 140

CAPEL GWLADYS ④

SPIRIT PATH

Nant Bryn-canol

SPIRIT PATH

N

③

Heol Adam
Roman Road

SPIRIT   PATH

Maen Cattwg

②

The Cross Inn

Nant
Cylla

Roman
Fort   GELLIGAER   ①

St Cattwg's Church   Motte

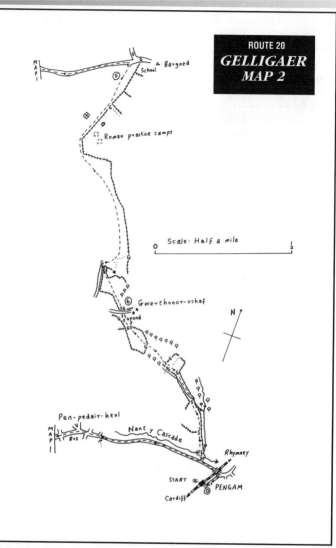

ROUTE 20
GELLIGAER
MAP 2

△ Bargoed
School
⑤
◇
Roman practice camps

Scale: Half a mile

G
⑥ Gwerthonor-uchaf
pond
N ↑

Pen-pedair-heol
Bus
Nant y Cascade
Rhymney
START
Cardiff
PENGAM

ground and fork right along a path which leads to Gelligaer **(Mile 1)**.

Take the path which passes St Cattwg's Church on your left and bears left through gates to the site of the Roman fort. Turn left at a lane and keep right along a road to pass the Cross Inn on your right. This is the Roman road Heol Adam. Shortly after passing under a power line, turn left across a stile and walk with a fence on your right **(Mile 2)**. Take a gate ahead and bear right to see the recumbent Maen Cattwg (with its cup markings).

Retrace your steps to Heol Adam, cross this road and continue over the stile opposite to go down the left-hand edge of a field. Take a gate in the corner and go ahead with a hedge on your right down to a stile. Cross this, bear left and reach another stile. Go ahead over this to walk with a hedge on your right. Ignore a gap in the hedge on your right but do bear right through a gap in the corner ahead and cut across the next field to a stile in its right-hand corner ahead. Bear right to another stile soon after it and walk with a fence on your left to a stile beside a gate **(Mile 3)**.

Go left to keep a fence on your right, cross a stream and go right to a track coming from Pen-pedair-heol which is aligned with Capel Gwladys. Go left to follow the path (and cross a road) to the Celtic cross marking the site of St Gwladys' chapel **(Mile 4)**.

Retrace your steps down to the road and go left along it towards Bargoed. Turn right before a junction and cattle grid. Follow a track which climbs to pass the sites of Roman practice camps behind a fence on your left **(Mile 5)**.

Continue to join a lane by crossing a cattle grid. Immediately after the cattle grid, turn left down to Gwerthonor-uchaf **(Mile 6)**. Keep descending with the waymarked path to cross a footbridge and reach the B4254 again. Go left to pass under the railway bridge and turn right to retrace your steps to Pengam railway station **(Mile 7)**.

EXPLORE THE WORLD
WITH A CICERONE GUIDE

Cicerone publishes over 280 guides for walking, trekking, climbing and exploring the UK, Europe and worldwide. Cicerone guides are available from outdoor shops, quality book stores and from the publisher.

Cicerone can be contacted on
www.cicerone.co.uk
www.ciceroneguides.com

OTHER CICERONE GUIDES FOR WALES

THE LLEYN PENINSULA COASTAL PATH   *John Cantrell.*
WALKING OFFA'S DYKE PATH   *David Hunter*
OWAIN GLYNDWR'S WAY   *Chris and Ronnie Catling*
THE PEMBROKESHIRE COASTAL PATH   *Dennis R. Kelsall*
SARN HELEN   *Arthur Rylance & John Cantrell*
THE SHROPSHIRE WAY   *Terry Marsh & Julie Meech*
WALKING DOWN THE WYE   *David Hunter*
A WELSH COAST TO COAST WALK Snowdonia to Gower   *John Gillham*
ASCENT OF SNOWDON   *E.G. Rowland*
ANGLESEY COAST WALKS   *Cecil Davies*
THE BRECON BEACONS   *Davies and Whittaker*
CLWYD ROCK   *Gary Dickinson*
HEREFORD AND THE WYE VALLEY   *David Hinchliffe*
HILL WALKING IN SNOWDONIA   *Steve Ashton*
HILLWALKING IN WALES Vol 1: Arans - Dovey Hills
HILLWALKING IN WALES Vol 2: Ffestiniog - Tarrens   *Peter Hermon*
THE MOUNTAINS OF ENGLAND AND WALES Vol 1: WALES   *John and Anne Nuttall*
THE RIDGES OF SNOWDONIA   *Steve Ashton*
SCRAMBLES IN SNOWDONIA   *Steve Ashton*
SEVERN WALKS   *David Hunter*
THE SHROPSHIRE HILLS - A Walker's Guide   *David Hunter*
SNOWDONIA WHITE WATER, SEA AND SURF - Canoe Guide   *Terry Storry*
WELSH WINTER CLIMBS   *Malcolm Campbell & Andy Newton*